My Father Knew the *Secret*

BRIAN PROCTOR

Permission should be addressed in writing to the author:
Brian Proctor, KellyProctorCo LLC: support@brianproctor.com

Published by:
KellyProctorCo LLC

ISBN-13: 979-8-9885800-0-3

First edition, 2023

Cover design by Trace Haskins
Interior design by Trace Haskins
Editing by Cory Kelly Proctor

Important Disclaimers

In my Dad's arms; 1962

DEDICATION

This book is dedicated to my father, Bob Proctor.

Bob Proctor was an extraordinary father, friend, and business partner. The stars aligned for me on the day I came into this world as his son.

My father's passion and dedication to sharing the information that changed his life, shaped my life, and changed the lives of countless others worldwide is timeless, and benefits any person that invests the time into studying it.

Bob Proctor was one of the great thinkers of our time.

I love you Dad, and miss you dearly.

ENDORSEMENTS

"This amazing book is loaded with timeless truths and eternal wisdom. Every page, every paragraph, contains insights and ideas that can be literally life-changing for you, in exactly the form you need, and at exactly the correct time for you. Put up your tray table and put on your seatbelt. You are about to enjoy one of the great experiences of life."

– Brian Tracy
President - Brian Tracy International

"...Brian writes from a unique angle, processing the wisdom he absorbed from his dad over the years and putting those key teachings into his own words. Bob Proctor's generosity was a wonderful blessing which came to me out of the blue, without any seeming effort on my part. Life often works that way. Brian explains how and why such gifts come to us or, more specifically, what you can do to make them happen."

– Price Pritchett, Ph.D.
Best-Selling Author of *You²: A High Velocity Formula for Multiplying your Personal Effectiveness in Quantum Leaps*

"This is one of my favorite books of all time! I couldn't put it down. It is truly a heartwarming story, filled with incredible inspirational life lessons and golden nuggets. I took pages of notes. This one is a 'must-read' for everyone. I LOVED IT!"

— Sonia Ricotti
#1 Best-Selling Author of *Unsinkable*
and the world's leading "Bounce Back" expert

"My Father Knew the Secret is heartwarming, brilliant, and, above all, insightful. This is the kind of book that will either get you moving again or take you from good to great. Brian has the same depth as his father and the same ability to speak so clearly, that both your heart and mind learn the lesson."

— Mike Dooley
NY Times Best-Selling Author of *Infinite Possibilities*

"Lovingly written! Apply one of the lessons Brian learned from Bob each day and let the brilliance of Bob Proctor become yours."

— Tina Lifford
Playwright, Actress and Author of *The Little Book of BIG LIES*

"I love this book! Bob Proctor personally changed my life and this book can change yours. Heartwarming, empowering, inspiring. A son's story of love for a man who lived The Secret, wrapped up in a self-help classic of wisdom. Just beautiful."

– Dr. Joe Vitale
Author *The Attractor Factor, Zero Limits, The Miracle* and more.

"I met Brian's Father, Bob Proctor, in January 1979. His teachings changed my life, for the better, in EVERY way. One of the blessings of meeting Bob, was also meeting his son Brian. Brian and I have been friends for many decades and I can speak from experience that Brian not only understands and shares his Dad's philosophies, he lives by these philosophies every day. I love that Brian created this incredible book to help you improve your life and achieve any dream you set for yourself. This book is one of the best books I have ever read, and I've read thousands of them. I highly recommend this book to my loved ones, friends and clients. I would suggest you invest in two copies; share one with a friend and study with them. You will find that will intensify the valuable lessons you will find contained these pages."

– Peggy McColl
New York Times Best Selling Author and Brian's friend

"Brian, you nailed it! It felt like I was reading a good novel; I didn't want to put it down once I started reading. You really captured not only your relationship with your Dad but how he lived. AND the cherry on top were the "points to consider" at the end of each chapter. This addition was pure genius as each reader has the opportunity to not only read interesting stories but also to learn the same lessons you learned from your Dad. I know he's proud! Congratulations."

— Linda Proctor
Bob Proctor's wife

"'My Father Knew the Secret' is my new favorite book of all time. Not only is it heartwarming and inspiring to read about Bob Proctor, a man who truly walked his talk. This book has given me a new perspective and lens for my life moving forward and makes me want to be a better, more kind person every day. This book really taught me so much and will be my go-to manual for manifesting. And for that, I am eternally grateful."

— Wendy Newman
Innertaining Media

8

"I absolutely loved reading 'My Father Knew the Secret'! This powerful and life-changing book masterfully captures the profound wisdom of Bob Proctor, beautifully shared through the perspective of his son, Brian Proctor. Whether you're new to Bob's teachings or a lifelong fan, this book is a must-read for anyone seeking personal growth, achievement, and the ability to make a profound contribution to the world. Prepare to be inspired and empowered to be unstoppable on your journey of growth and success."

— Cynthia Kersey
Best-Selling Author of *Unstoppable*,
Founder & CEO, Unstoppable Foundation

"I knew and worked alongside Bob Proctor for many years. What his son Brian has written in 'My Father Knew the Secret' reveals the man behind the name and makes clear why Bob was loved by so many. His life's work was transformational, and Brian shares precisely how that work shaped and affected him. It is a unique perspective that anyone will benefit from. Apply the lessons in this book and your life will never be the same."

—Jack Canfield
Co-author of the Best-Selling *Chicken Soup for the Soul* series
and *The Success Principles*

"It's not often that I have the opportunity to read a book that confirms my belief that love makes the world go round. I've known Brian and his dad for many years and Brian's book about his relationship with his father Bob Proctor is a profoundly honest and uplifting recounting of the immense impact Bob's love for learning and teaching has had on everyone he's ever touched. Buy this book share this book and most importantly find ways to honor the 'Secret' Bob spent his incredible life bringing to life."

— Blaine Bartlett
Best-Selling Author of *Compassionate Capitalism:*
A Journey to the Soul of Business

"In these pages Brian Proctor shares intimate stories, insights, and lessons about his father, Bob Proctor, one of the most influential thought leaders of his time. This book will help you become aware of the unlimited potential already inside of all of us. How to think and dream big, stretching yourself beyond what you think you are capable of. Thank you Brian for sharing your Father with the World."

— Robert Pascuzzi
Best-Selling Author, Film Producer, and Entrepreneur

TABLE OF CONTENTS

FOREWORD

The title truthfully frames this book —
Bob Proctor knew the secret.

In fact, he wrapped his life around it, personally lived the secret, and shared it with people across Planet Earth. It's powerful stuff. Bob changed countless millions of lives in so many positive ways.

Brian Proctor, the author and probably the world's #1 expert on his dad, knows the secret too. In spades.

In the following pages you'll see that Brian writes from a unique angle, processing the wisdom he absorbed from his dad over the years and putting those key teachings into his own words. The book is part biography, part memoir, and part a son's loving "pay it forward" message in gratitude to his world renowned father. It's an inspiring, heartfelt story. And it, too, has the power to change your life.

I first came to know Bob and Brian from afar.

I had written a small handbook titled *You²*, a concise set of counterintuitive rules for making quantum leaps in performance. It grew out of the dissertation research for my Ph.D. in psychology plus my years of consulting to major corporations on fast growth. Large orders for the handbook kept coming from a firm in Toronto. In fact, that outfit seemed to be doing a better job of promoting it than we ourselves were doing here in Dallas! So, I chased down the phone number, called to see who this was, and discovered that *You²* was one of Bob Proctor's favorite books. He continued to showcase it until he passed into the great beyond.

Bob Proctor's generosity was a wonderful blessing which came to me out of the blue, without any seeming effort on my part.

Life often works that way. Brian explains how and why such gifts come to us or, more specifically, what you can do to make them happen. This is part of the secret he reveals in the pages to come.

You can open the book anywhere, start reading, and find teachings that will enrich your life and seriously enlarge your achievements.

Brian writes in an easy conversational style, but the message has true gravity. I challenge you to study it. Do the exercises. Live the lessons. Your life will shift to a higher plane of performance, and you will contribute more to your world.

As a licensed psychologist, I assure you that the behavioral fundamentals in Brian's book are solid. I will also tell you, without any doubt or hesitation, that you possess great untapped potential. It lies silent within you, ready to be released, just waiting for you to move on your best ambitions.

In this book Brian shows you how to move.

Now go!

– Price Pritchett, Ph.D.
CEO – PRITCHETT, LP and Author of the
You2 Quantum Leap Strategies series and more

INTRODUCTION

The title of this book holds a lot of truth. My father did know the secret. He lived that secret up to his last breath.

For sixty years, I went to school on Bob Proctor's experiences and wisdom, and for nearly thirty of those years, I worked by his side. Those years with Bob Proctor as my father and friend gave me a unique understanding that I feel a sincere responsibility to share.

For most of my life, the question I have been asked most often is, "What is it like having Bob Proctor as a father?" So, my answer to that question is what you hold here.

I am one of the few who saw Bob Proctor work in the self-development industry from the beginning. I was there with him through it all. I saw how hard he worked crafting his message, always wanting to get it just right so that anyone could understand and benefit regardless of their education, background, or culture. He genuinely strived to make a difference in this world.

I began writing this book in 2019, and on many occasions, Dad would say to me, "Brian, don't rush it. Take your time and write from your heart. The book will be done when it is supposed to be." A part of me wonders if he knew he would not be here when I was finished. I know he enjoyed our conversations about this book, and I suspect that he didn't want that to end.

When Dad got sick, I set this project aside and went home to Toronto to be with him and his wife Linda, helping however I could. Then, when I thought he was better, I resumed writing. Though that only lasted a couple of months. It wasn't long before I found myself back in Toronto. This time sitting at his bedside in the hospital.

Bob Proctor was wise, different than most. He possessed an understanding that came from his years of persistence and constant study. From that understanding, Dad had a peaceful knowing that put him in a class all his own.

Over the years, I accumulated stacks of notebooks from Dad's seminars, each intertwined with my thoughts on his teachings. These notebooks, my conversations with my father, and my 60 years of life experiences growing up with him became the template for this book.

I hope that what I share here helps you as much as it has helped shape and guide me. I always expected this book to be published and released while Dad was alive. But that didn't happen. Instead, it happened when it was supposed to happen.

I feel my Dad's presence every day. I imagine him now enjoying his new journey, likely speaking from the stage in heaven.

HOW TO USE THIS BOOK

Important Tips From The Author

The lessons you will find in this book are simple. They tie into and revolve around creating value in relationships.

The success I experience today is due to the relationships I have cultivated based on what I have learned from growing up with Bob Proctor as my father. Not just my relationships with those around me but, most importantly, my relationship with myself.

I have learned that the deeper you can love yourself, the easier it is to love and appreciate others. No matter what is happening around you, the world is better when you come from a place of love.

In this book, you will find stories and thoughts to trigger your thinking. In addition, you will find ideas for questioning your perspective and ways to improve your life and relationships.

I learned from my father that whenever I was having an issue or needed an answer, I could take out a book that I was studying and just let it open onto a page and start reading. He said that the answer I was looking for would usually reveal itself. So that is how I have written this book. You can pick this up, open it anywhere, and find something wise that my father taught me. I know in my heart something here will resonate with you, and when you read that message, you will know.

Use these lessons in whatever way you need. And trust that when you start living your life with awareness and through conscious choices, every part of your life will improve, and when that happens, everyone around you will benefit. It is a beautiful ripple effect.

In July 2014, we held a spectacular 80th birthday party for Dad at his favorite hotel – The Bellagio in Las Vegas. It was during that party that my Uncle Al stood at the front of the ballroom with a microphone and said to the crowd gathered, "When my big brother went on his journey all those years ago, it improved the lives of everyone around him - his siblings, his kids, nieces, nephews, and those who were fortunate to call him a friend. It was like throwing a pebble into the water and watching the vibrational change of the water when it hit."

Dad's journey is now being shared with the fourth generation of Proctors. He has altered paradigms in our family that will continue forever. And you have the capacity to be that person too – for you and your family. You can be the one that changes everything for the better.

As you read these pages, please keep an open mind and be willing to question your beliefs and how they serve you (or don't) in your day-to-day life.

At the end of most chapters in this book, you will find thinking points to *'consider'* related to that chapter and space to write notes. Use those sections provided and make this book your personal roadmap by highlighting what resonates with you and putting it into practice.

Return to this book often to remind yourself how you want to live. And if you are a student of Bob Proctor's, you know that repetition through reading creates change. You can't help but get emotionally involved with an idea when you are reading it over and over. My father was a testament to that. I promise that when you do this, your world will brighten. The trees will look greener, and you will hear the birds sing louder. Every day will be better. And as Dad often said, "Better is a good word."

Honor who you are today and imagine how you can improve. You are where you are right now because of past decisions and circumstances. That is a fact that you cannot change, so honor it. And know that you can choose and cultivate who you become from this moment forward.

A good practice would be to date the responses you write throughout this book, so you can use the yardstick of time to track your growth whenever you return to a chapter.

I do know how fortunate I am to call Bob Proctor my father. This book is my way of sharing that privilege with you. And it is a way for me to honor who Bob Proctor is to me. It is a way for me to keep his memory alive.

CONSIDER...

- *If all your past experiences make you who you are today, then who would you be if you forgot your past and started in a new place?*

- *What if the only thing you knew was that you could be, do, or have anything you truly desired? What would you want to be, do, or have?*

- *What will happen in your life if you show up as the best version of yourself?*

NOTES:

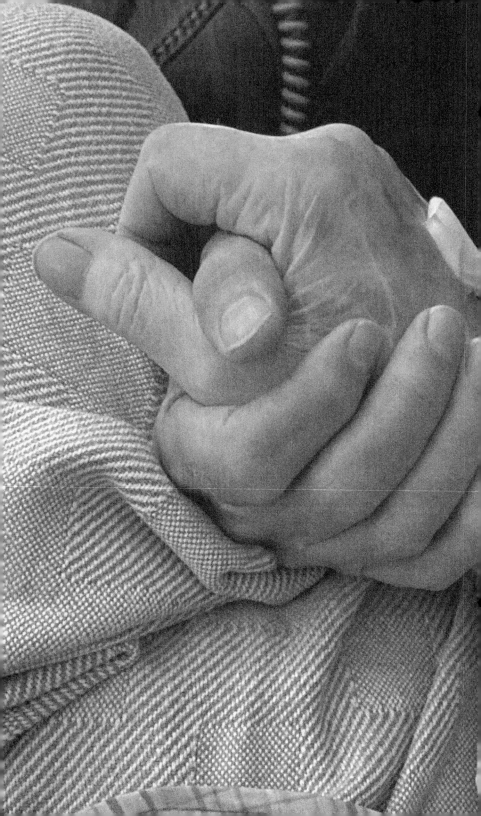

CHAPTER 1

DAD'S FINAL LESSON

Saying Goodbye

The night of February 3, 2022, will be forever etched in my mind. That was the evening that my father passed away. I consider myself fortunate to have been there holding his hand when he made his transition. I've been through difficult things in my life, but nothing compares to saying goodbye to my Dad.

I was with my father for much of his last six months of life. And what we shared was precious and deeply meaningful - I learned so much. It was as if Dad wanted to ensure I got it all before he left. We talked and reminisced for hours each day, often in the early mornings like we had done on the phone for many years - that was our time.

My father was a man who freely gave and took pride in helping others. He took an interest in everyone he encountered. If you are one of those people who had the chance to meet him either at an event or online, or maybe it was a phone call, you know what I mean. At seminar events, I would often escort him through the event venue to ensure we got him back on stage on time. So often, people would catch him in the hallway or on an elevator and he would always stop, shake hands, perhaps take a picture and most importantly - he would give you time. You will always remember having met Bob Proctor. However, as available as he was to everyone, his family was always closest to his heart.

The night of his passing on February 3, 2022, he was surrounded by his wife Linda, my sister Colleen, my brother Raymond, me, and our spouses, plus a dear friend who was there to help guide us and make it as comfortable as possible for Dad.

My father always knew what he wanted and would do whatever it took to achieve that. Being surrounded by family is how he wanted to go, and right to the end, he knew how to make it happen.

Only a few days earlier, when we were in the hospital, it was clear that the end was coming. Dad knew he would be leaving us and was adamant about coming home. No - was not an answer he would accept. Dad focused only on making it happen. At that point, he was in the Intensive Care Unit and his visitor list was extremely limited. My father needed to see, touch, and say goodbye to his eleven grandchildren personally, along with some special friends.

As you can imagine, he was not doing very well. But despite this, he continued to make anyone in his presence feel special. He was true to his being right until the very end. While we were waiting together in his hospital room for the transport team to arrive, we held hands, and he was smiling. I could feel his energy. The ambulance attendants soon came with a gurney to begin the process of transporting him home. When the two men walked into the room, Dad was so happy that he was going home that he lit up at the sight of them. As anxious as he was to get this process going, he did what you would expect Bob Proctor to do. He made these two men feel seen. It was a powerful reminder of a great principle that my father lived by.

Dad looked at the first gentleman and said, "Wait, first tell me, what's your name?" He answered, "Mohammad." Dad looked him in the eye and with a smile said, "Mohammad is a powerful name." He then looked at the second man and asked him the same question. He replied, "Tourag." Dad said, "I love that name; unique and strong!" Both men paused and stood there for a moment, looking at my father. They had no idea who he was, but Dad had put a smile on both their faces. He was wrapping them in kindness.

That kindness he showed those two men caused them to be even kinder to him, which was nice. They gently moved him to the stretcher and were about to wheel him out when Dad did something I will never forget.

He put his arms up in the air and said, "Mohammad, Tourag, take me home boys!" He said it with such enthusiasm that he surprised all of us. What an incredible frame of mind to be in when making your final journey home. It was unbelievable and extraordinary all at the same time.

Dad was also kind to the nurses, doctors, and orderlies. Anyone that came into his room left feeling different. He was calm and caring and constantly told whomever he came in contact with that they were doing a good job even as they did the necessary poking and prodding.

I can tell you Dad was not big on being in a hospital and all that it entailed, but he didn't let it bother him, and he always made it easier for the healthcare workers trying to help him.

At one point, a nurse who needed to add another IV was apologizing to my father for having difficulty finding a vein. He touched her lightly and said, "You just do whatever you need to do. It's ok. You're doing a great job."

I was so proud to be by his side, watching the way he talked to the people caring for him while he lay there, not feeling well and, quite frankly, in extreme discomfort. But here is a big takeaway that will always be with me. Dad did not let his current adverse circumstances dictate how he would treat those around him.

The night Dad was escorted out of the hospital by Mohammad and Tourag, there was a lineup of teary-eyed hospital staff waiting for him, wanting to touch him and say goodbye. After he passed, we received notes from the people working in the hospital telling us what a great man he was and how he made them feel at his toughest moment in life. He had made a real impression on these people whom he had only met for a moment in time, but that is how he lived his life to the very end.

In his worst moments, Dad looked for the good around him. Even in those last few days when his pain was extreme, he saw only the good and made sure that he told anyone in his world how special they were. My father never saw the point in talking about or focusing on the negative side of things. Looking for the good in everything is how he lived.

Dad believed in what he liked to call - the Impression of Increase. The theory is to have every person you meet feel better because they were in your presence. Bob Proctor was a master at this. When teaching from the stage, you would watch him come down into the audience and touch someone lightly on the shoulder as he spoke to them. He would make that person feel like they were the only one in the room. That is an extraordinary thing. Feeling seen and understood is a universal need, and Dad understood that assignment.

In Bob Proctor's many recordings, you will hear him say, "A pro is at their best regardless." I witnessed that firsthand during this time. Dad was a pro, regardless. He was a pro to his last breath. To give this context, you should know that his last six months were tough. He was in a lot of pain and in and out of the hospital. Because of that pain, he mostly used a wheelchair at the end. He could take a few steps, but it wasn't easy.

On top of that, he had had several infections that significantly weakened him. As a result, we spent most of our time together, quietly talking. I could feel his need to share as much with me as possible.

As you likely know, Bob Proctor loved to teach. Nothing was more important to him than sharing his message, knowing it could help someone live a better life. He knew this because he had changed his own life with this material. He wasn't about to let his condition stop him now. He still had so much he wanted to share. So we made sure we were there to help him do just that.

During those last few months, it would often take many hours to navigate his pain and get him dressed so he could get in front of the camera and share his message. Dad loved fashion and had a lot of style - he was in a class all his own. My father was well known for his suits, ties and Italian shoes. His closet was lined with custom-made suits from Toronto and custom-made shoes from Italy. It looked like an art exhibit. On filming days, it would take both Linda and I and sometimes my son Danny to prepare him for a broadcast. We all worked to get everything chosen and adjusted to his satisfaction. We had a lot of laughs together, trying to get him ready, with Dad's laugh despite his discomfort always being the loudest of all.

The studio where my father broadcasted from was 100 steps from the house. He loved his studio; it was his place to create.

When Dad was dressed and ready, we'd walk those 100 steps together. Usually, with me on one side and Danny on the other. Once he was situated at his desk and the camera went live he forgot all his pain and spoke with incredible strength as if channeling the information to the viewers watching.

If you saw any of his live broadcasts at the end of his life, the odds are you did not know he was in pain. His desire to reach as many people as possible with his message was intense. And at the end, that desire became more urgent. He might only teach for 30 minutes. But he would be on fire for those 30 minutes, always at his best when it counted.

When he would finish, Danny and I would help him up and back into the house. Dad never complained, but you could see the pain on his face. He would lie on the couch in the sitting room and rest for hours. Sometimes while lying there, when I thought he was asleep, he would suddenly say, "Hey Bri, isn't this a great life? Look at this beautiful room; even the ceiling is beautiful." Always living from a place of gratitude.

Seeing him in this pain was heartbreaking. I would often lay in bed at night during this time and marvel with a sense of sorrow at how he could sustain such a good attitude and humor. His strength, attitude and determination during those last months were remarkable.

As a father, my Dad did everything he could to take care of us all. Throughout my life, I watched him give the same love and care to his audience and clients. But, in the end, his last gift was that we could take care of him. I remember whispering that in his ear near the end and telling him how much I loved him.

At that point, he could not communicate very well with words and would drift in and out of consciousness, but I knew he could hear and understand me. When I would whisper in his ear, he would give my hand a gentle squeeze. He was mentally sharp, but his body was letting go. Squeezing my hand was his way of thanking me and letting me know he was there.

Sometimes when Dad appeared to be asleep, he would suddenly make a motion that he wanted you to hold his hand.

One of the last things my Dad said to me was, "Brian, I will always be with you. Talk to me every day. Ask me questions when you talk to me, and the answers will come to you." He said this many times to me and made sure I understood.

I can see his loving face while lying there, willing me to understand that he will always be with me. That vision gives me strength.

Bob Proctor was the most extraordinary, loving, kind, and giving man I have ever known. He walked his talk, and I have witnessed that my entire life. I am fortunate to have had 60 years with him by my side. And I am incredibly grateful for that.

I want you to understand that he was not afraid of dying. He was able to say goodbye to all his family and close friends. And the best thing was that he did it his way.

Listen To Your Inner Voice

My father is a direct link to the modern science of success that is so popular today. He was studying and teaching personal growth long before it was popular, driven by a desire to help people understand and tap into the potential of their mind in order to live a life of prosperity, rewarding relationships, and greater awareness of what lies within them and around them.

In his final days, when my father so desperately wanted me to understand that he would always be with me, I promised him I understood.

He said I should continue to ask him questions as if we were having a conversation and that to understand the answer, I would need to get into a quiet place and calm my mind and that in this relaxed state, I would know. I would feel the answer and likely call it my intuition. He told me to allow that to guide me.

Currently, I am going through a business situation that feels wrong. My intuition is screaming at me. In the past, I may have passed that off as nonsense or fear.

Not anymore. This last lesson from my father, the one he worked so hard to make sure I understood, is likely one of the most important.

I will listen to that inner voice and follow it. I choose to let that inner voice represent my father speaking to me. Whether it is or not - is irrelevant. I know that if I follow my heart and pay attention, this awareness will always guide me in the right direction.

Now, my advice to you is to do the same. Always seek out and listen to your inner voice. No matter what is happening in or around you. If you can relax, quiet your mind and start asking questions, the answers will come. Let that voice speak with great tenderness. Sometimes those answers might not be convenient. However, if we pay attention and let it guide us from a place of inner peace, I firmly believe we will be on track for a life with more meaning and less regret.

Know as I do that Bob Proctor's wisdom is always here with us. Do your part and commit to a life of curiosity and learning. Question the way you reflexively do things. Our reactions and responses are likely our paradigms that are a part of our belief system, which may be an assumed truth. So, get curious and question, and always choose growth.

The Last Page

"Personal development has no finish line."
— Bob Proctor

I know that my father took that phrase to heart. He studied right up to the week of his passing. He was forever reading and sharing ideas. He never thought he knew it all. He always felt there was still so much to discover and learn. Near the end of his life, I would sit and read to him. Sometimes, when I thought he was asleep, he would suddenly say, "Read that again."

My father's desire for growth indeed had no finish line, and more than anything, he wanted to pass on that knowledge. He wanted everyone to understand that a lifelong thirst and commitment to growth through study and understanding is the key to expanding our mind. Combining that understanding with action is the path to discovering our untapped potential.

I remember him saying something from the stage that got a good laugh but also showed how important he thought this was and how much he wanted you to understand it. He said, "If I could take all this information, bottle it up into a shot and inject you in the ass with it, I would."

That desire and passion were with him right to the end.

Christmas 2021

When I go into his studio now, the book in his book holder is *The Hidden Power by Thomas Troward*, which is open to the two pages he was studying. Many of the words are highlighted in yellow.

The Hidden Power was written long ago, so the writing is less current than today's ideals. However, each page has a valuable lesson and is as relevant as ever.

I have no idea how long my father was on those two pages, but it wasn't unusual for him to study the same page for months. He always took his time to make sure he fully understood a concept. That is a form of learning that takes extraordinary patience and persistence. But, because he studied this way, he had a depth of knowledge and an understanding that few have.

When Dad resonated with an author, he would incorporate what he was studying until it became a part of his new paradigm. He was still doing this at the age of 87. Learning excited him; his curiosity was insatiable. That is a big part of what made him different and why he had such a large following. You could feel his passion, and when he taught, he communicated in a way that made the concepts easy to understand. It didn't matter where you lived, what culture you came from, or what language you spoke, Bob Proctor, like no other, got you excited about your life and the possibilities before you.

CONSIDER...

- *If you were to model Bob Proctor's way of life and philosophy about daily study, how much could you achieve during the rest of your lifetime on Earth?*

- *My father used to highlight that in order to succeed, one must ask themselves these questions:*

  1) Am I willing?
  2) Am I able?

- *Are you willing and able to commit to daily study? Even just reading a paragraph a day adds up over a lifetime!*

NOTES:

CHAPTER 2

ATTRACTION

The Movie That Changed Everything

*"The Universe wants us to have an abundant life,
and it is always supporting us in
making this a reality."*
– Bob Proctor

Bob Proctor expected big things would happen for him. When I say big, I mean something that would shift his business in a way that would forever change the way he did things and help him to reach and impact more people than he ever had.

It was because Dad studied every day that he expected something big to happen. It was an inner knowing developed because of the knowledge he had acquired and applied since he was given a copy of Think and Grow Rich for the first time on October 21, 1961. I was born in December of that same year - this journey has been my entire life.

It was 2005 when something very big did indeed arrive; it was the opportunity to be in a movie titled *The Secret*. By this time,

Dad had been in the personal and professional development space for 45 years. He had been traveling, giving seminars and teaching in boardrooms all over the world. And he'd already spent years working his tail off in an effort to reach more people and change more lives. And for many of those years, he was gone much more than he was home. There were even years when he was flying from Toronto to Kuala Lumpur, the capital of Malaysia, every three weeks to work with the Malaysian Airlines group.

Being in the personal and professional development realm for this long, Dad was a walking example of the material he taught. But it was *The Secret* that propelled Bob Proctor and his message to millions of people and onto a worldwide stage seemingly overnight. This opportunity, its massive popularity, and how it came about changed everything for Dad. What I love about this story is that the movie is based on the Law of Attraction, and for me there is no better example of the Law of Attraction than how my father came to be in that movie.

It was in the spring of 2005; Dad was in an airport between flights and called his long-time friend and executive assistant, Gina Hayden. Gina, at that time, had worked closely with Dad for twenty years. They often spoke multiple times a day. He called Gina because his voicemail was full of messages, and he needed her help clearing them. One voice message, specifically, was broken up and difficult to understand. He thought it was a number from Australia and that it might have been from someone named Glenda; it was about a movie.

After clearing Dad's voicemails, Gina called him back to discuss an interesting conversation she had just had with the woman named Glenda from Australia. Glenda is the sister of Rhonda Byrne, who is the creator of *The Secret*. Glenda told Gina that a film crew from Australia was shooting a movie, and they would like to have Bob Proctor in it. She said the crew planned to return to Australia in a few weeks but were shooting in Aspen, Colorado, the following weekend and had been trying to reach Bob Proctor for over a month. Well, it just so happened that Dad was doing a seminar in Aspen that very same weekend. So, all he would have to do was walk from one hotel and across the road to another. So, Rhonda's team added Bob Proctor to their filming line-up, and Dad added the time to his itinerary.

When Dad arrived in Aspen and sat down to meet the film crew for the first time, he realized they had done their research and knew he had been in this business for a long time. The movie was to be based on 'The Little Green Book,' which happened to be *The Science of Getting Rich by Wallace Wattles*. Well, Dad knew this book intimately. The Science of Getting Rich, along with many other books, had been in his daily study rotation for over 40 years. So, he knew it inside and out and often taught many of the principles Wattles wrote about. In fact, this was the book that had been introduced to him by one of his mentors, Lloyd Conant.

The crew gave him a brief overview of what they were aiming for. Dad did not enjoy working with teleprompters, so he instead had them ask him questions. After he'd answered all their questions, he asked if he could record something for them – unscripted.

He suggested they could use or not use it; it was up to them. Then he spoke from the heart about everything he had studied and taught for the prior 45 years. If you have ever seen Bob Proctor on stage, you know how information flows to and through him. And that is precisely what happened that afternoon in that hotel room in Aspen, Colorado. He recorded a 20-minute piece on The Law of Attraction in one take. It was flawless. The crew was blown away. They loved the additional footage so much that they offered it as a bonus segment on the DVD. My father was back in his room across the street in just over an hour.

Months later, when Rhonda's team had finished editing *The Secret*, Rhonda sent a DVD of the movie to Toronto. That DVD sat on the counter in Dad and Linda's house for weeks until finally, Dad said to Linda, "We really should watch this." When they finished watching it, Dad knew immediately that this movie would impact millions of people. He turned to Linda and said, "This is going to be bigger than any of us can imagine." And he was right.

Another interesting piece of this story is that Rhonda did not have funds to pay the people who agreed to be in the movie. Yet, in true Bob Proctor fashion, he didn't care about that - what he wanted was to get this message out to a larger audience. Other teachers were asked to be in *The Secret* but declined when they learned they wouldn't be compensated for their time. But Dad lived his life following Universal Laws and understood the Law of Cause and Effect; he knew that what you send out comes back. He lived focused on the CAUSE, and let the EFFECT show up.

Dad didn't get paid for that hour in Aspen. But he sure got rewarded. Bob Proctor stood out in that movie, his authenticity resonated with millions, and suddenly the phone began ringing off the hook. He became known as one of the world's most significant Law of Attraction experts. As such, he was invited to speak all over the world and was also invited to be on several television shows - Larry King Live (twice), The Ellen DeGeneres Show, and Nightline. Dad's stock had gone through the roof. Promoters worldwide were calling and wanting him to speak - Colombia, China, Peru, Romania, Brazil, everyone wanted Bob Proctor. He was ready. In fact, he'd been waiting for this. He'd been – EXPECTING.

The Secret resulted from an inspired idea that Rhonda Byrne had and acted on. She accomplished exactly what she set out to accomplish. *The Secret* touched and changed the lives of millions of people, and it raised awareness around the idea that we all work with one infinite power and are guided by the same Laws of the Universe. By focusing that movie on The Law of Attraction, Rhonda raised collective consciousness around the concept that what we are thinking and holding in our mind, we are attracting.

When I think of how Dad lived his life, I know he was in the frequency needed to attract everything that happened to put him across the street from that hotel in Colorado, on the same weekend Rhonda Byrne's team was filming. Especially since, at the age of 72 - he had only been in Aspen one other time; this was not a regular stop for him. And yet, there he was.

My father was always working towards bigger goals and after already working in this industry for 45 years, there is no doubt in my mind that he had attracted this opportunity to him.

He had worked his entire adult life for this. However, it was the release of the movie *The Secret* that set a new and different beginning for him; his business and life were never the same.

Visiting Victoria, British Columbia
with my wife, Cory

Finding Lasting Love

"Understand that the good that you desire is already here. What you must do is get in harmony with it. And you do that with your thinking."
— *Bob Proctor*

For much of my life, I'd had an up-and-down love life. As difficult as the failures were, I knew my path was a necessary lesson. By the time I was in my fifties, I wasn't sure if a true love story was in the cards for me. I knew I couldn't do anything to change what had occurred in my past. And I did my best to harvest the good from those experiences and move forward with confidence that I was building a better life because of what I had learned.

Of course, my two children, Danny and Leanne, have been a blessing. Expanding my world in ways I could never have imagined and connecting me to a deep feeling of pleasure, meaning, and purpose. The joy of being their father is my proof that it doesn't matter how bad some things were; I received the gift of two wonderful, beautiful children who positively impacted everything about my life.

After my kids were grown and following the end of a particularly tough relationship I'd been in, I took a long break from dating. I even took a break from thinking about having a woman in my life. Taking that time gave me space to build a life in a way that forced me to consider what I truly wanted and to get clear on what's important to me.

Moving forward with my plan to work on myself took a lot of self-reflection and inner work that wasn't always easy. First, I had to identify what I truly wanted for my life without a partner. Defining that helped me gain clarity and to set boundaries. Next, I needed to work on putting myself first, which was also challenging, but I came to know myself better through that process.

I moved to Florida and chose to live in an area where I had often taken vacations. I embraced a new world, and the change was good for my soul. It wasn't always easy, but I knew I wanted a clean slate. I needed to become a better version of myself and create new habits. My old patterns were not working, and it was time for me to ask myself why. I needed to come back to what I knew and begin thinking from a place of what I wanted rather than what had been.

Slowly, after a lot of self-work, I began to feel the desire to be in an honest and loving relationship again. I wanted a woman to love and appreciate and I wanted someone who would love and appreciate me back - for who I was. I deeply desired a genuinely caring, loving, and lasting partnership.

In seminars, during the question-and-answer session, you could count on someone raising their hand and asking Dad about finding genuine and lasting love. His answer was always simple and easy to follow.

He would give an exercise to take a sheet of paper and draw a circle on it, and in that circle, write, my man or my woman - whichever it is you want to attract. Next, you make it look like a starburst with many lines projecting from the circle. Then you write along the lines the qualities you want in a partner and relationship and be very clear. He would add that the first thing you want is for this person to be free and happy - because if they are not, you won't be either.

We are all expressions of the same power and can only attract what we are in harmonious vibration with. So, this exercise helps you to get clear. You do not put a face on your person. Dad would say this because if you are making this about a specific person, you are messing with their mind, and you do not have a right to do that. You also need to visualize yourself with this person as well as feel what it will be like to spend time together. You could do this by tapping into the love you feel in your heart when you are with someone or something you care about.

Doing this exercise puts you in the right vibration to attract the person you are in harmony with. And being clear brings focus. It makes your choices and actions intentional.

So now it was my time to put that exercise into practice and try it for myself. First, I wrote out in detail my perfect partner. Then, I created a simple Word document and put it on my desktop computer. I decided that rather than a physical description, I would write out what her personality was like, what her morals were, what she enjoyed, and so on. I wrote the things that were important to me. This also became an exercise in boundaries because it helped me clarify what was unacceptable by writing the opposite. Seeing that in writing really helped me to define my limits.

Every morning I would open the document and read it. I read it with the awareness that the woman I was looking for was on her way. I found myself adding to the document regularly as ideas hit me. I put things like how she would love me and how she would treat me. I also added how I would love and treat her. I began to have fun with it and got excited with anticipation. I also deleted things that became less important as I got clearer. I got to where I looked forward to reviewing this every day because I felt that, for the first time, I was getting in harmony with a higher relationship standard that I was defining.

I also started writing in my gratitude journal about how grateful I was that this woman was finding her way to me. I freely allowed everything to flow and did not force anything.

I became so intimate with my graphic and list that when I went on a date, I knew immediately if the woman I was sitting across from was even close to what I was looking for. I might not have looked as closely if I had not been so aware of what I wanted. As a result, I had several first and-only dates. I felt empowered rather than defeated because I knew what I was looking for and had decided never to settle again.

For years at our events, I would sit next to a woman I worked with within our company. Her name was Cory, and she lived in Alaska. I clearly remember the first time I met her in 2012.

It was 2014 when we were placed together at events. I realized later exactly how we ended up at our little table together. It was my father. Dad fell in love with Cory right from the start. He would say to me, "She thinks differently."

It was during an event in Los Angeles that Dad decided he needed to be able to see key people from his team while he was on stage. People that he could make eye contact with and confirm that the promises he was making from the stage were being noted and followed through on.

In short order, Dad had orchestrated that a table would always be just to the left of the stage. It would be out of the bright lights and close enough that he could see who was sitting there. Then, he decided that Cory and I would be the two people sitting there. Our table always had a third chair where Dad could sit for a break when he gave the audience an exercise. Putting us together at that table deepened my friendship with Cory. I know now that was intentional. Dad often saw what I needed before I did. It was that way for many people in his life. He would patiently wait for us to see what he already knew.

Cory and I celebrating the start of 2020 with my Dad and Gina Hayden in Las Vegas

Cory and I would go for walks in the morning before the seminars started and discuss what was happening in each other's lives. It was always easy and comfortable. We would see each other once every two months or so. We created an easy friendship and got to know each other.

I was very interested in her but wanted to avoid crossing any lines since we worked together. So, in my eyes, she was off limits. We had easy chemistry, but it didn't go any further because of work.

In 2016, I was staying at my brother Ray's house in Toronto. I clearly remember driving one day and talking with a very good friend, my father's assistant, Gina Hayden. I shared with Gina how much I would love to go on a trip to Italy to celebrate my 55th birthday, but I wanted to go with someone special.

At that time, I had no one special in my life. Gina suggested I call a woman we both knew and invite her. I told her that I was not interested in that person. I said there was someone else I would love to go with but felt I couldn't. I remember exactly where I was because of Gina's response.

She said, "It's Cory, isn't it?"

I have no idea why she said that or how she knew how I felt about Cory. I instantly responded, "I can't because we work together."

Gina convinced me that I should let Cory know how I felt. From that moment on, it was all I could think about. I knew Cory as a friend, and from what I knew of her, she certainly fit my description in my ideal partner document.

When I returned to Florida, I finally got the courage to call her to tell her how I felt. Her first response was, "I like you too, Brian," and that was it. She said it in a way that reflected a friendship only, so I hung up feeling dejected. As I sat there, I relived our conversation and concluded that she didn't understand the context of what I was saying.

So, I called her back and was more explicit. I knew by her awkward silence that I'd surprised her. Then, finally, she said, "Brian, I live in Alaska, and you are in Florida. How in the world would we make that work?" I knew at that moment that she was interested in me. I even surprised myself with my response. I said, "Cory, if you are interested in me, let's not worry about how it would work. Let's see how things go and how we feel as we progress." I could feel the words from my father's seminars coming through me. "Don't worry about the how. Just decide what you want; the how will reveal itself."

I asked her if we could speak every day on the phone. I knew it would be good to keep a connection between seeing each other at events, and talking each day would help us get to know each other in a different way. She agreed, and I knew that was a big commitment for her. Our friendship had brought to light that she did not particularly like to talk on the phone, plus our time zones put us 4 hours apart. But this is when the magic started to happen.

The more I got to know Cory through those daily phone calls, and then when we spent time together, I realized that she was exactly what I had described in my document. The only thing that did not fit was that I wanted to find someone who lived in the same state. So, I decided the geography was unimportant. We would figure that out.

As I write this, I am smiling, thinking about how easy it was once I got clear. I think my father was as happy as I was when Cory and I got together.

I remember when I told Dad that we were getting married. He was delighted. I then said to him that Cory and I had decided that we were going to have a small private ceremony in Hawaii with only our kids present. That we were not inviting guests or additional family. We wanted to use this opportunity to bond our families together. We rented a house that was large enough for all the kids and us, and we scheduled an official to perform a sunrise ceremony at 6:30 am. Cory and I are both morning people, and this idea really suited us.

Well, Bob Proctor does not hear the word – "no" – when he really wants something. He made sure that he was at that ceremony and witnessed the entire thing. He had even prepared a piece that he read, and it was beautiful. I am forever grateful that Dad was there and that he didn't hear the word – "no". Funny enough, we are still trying to explain this to my mother and Cory's parents.

Today Cory and I are married and living a caring, loving relationship – a true love story. Creating that document clarified what I wanted, and I discovered that what I was looking for had been sitting right beside me.

CONSIDER...

Are you looking for true love?

If you are attracting what you don't want, you better take a look at yourself because you are the only person you can change; you can never change another person. Do the inner work first and become what you want to attract into your life. You don't attract what you want; you attract what you are. Get clear on what you want and how you want to be treated. Only in clarity will you be able to recognize and attract what you are, want, and deserve.

Do the exercise.

If you want to attract someone special that elevates your world, the exercise my father gave is essential. So, get a piece of paper and begin now.

- *Draw the circle.*
- *Add the starburst lines.*
- *Add the qualities.*
- *Refine each day and bring clarity to your thoughts.*
- *Think about your vision several times each day.*
- *Feel yourself in this relationship.*
- *Don't compromise.*

NOTES:

We Become What We Think About

*"Do you want to know what you are
thinking about most of the time?
Take a look at the results you are getting.
Your results will tell you exactly what your
dominating thoughts are."
– Bob Proctor*

I learned from a young age to be in control of my thoughts. Dad would teach me to bring my attention back to what I was thinking. He would do this by asking me to look at my thoughts with fascination. To sort of detach from my thinking mind and examine what my thoughts were and then try to link that to what was happening in my world. He would then encourage me to connect the dots.

Learning to live from the inside out by choosing and focusing on thoughts that align with my goals and desires instead of letting the outside world dictate what I think and feel has been a lifelong exercise. It comes down to awareness: the ability to recognize when my thoughts, actions, and emotions are not aligning with my goals and desires.

By being hyper-vigilant of my thoughts, I have learned to shift my vibration and open myself up to attract and create the results

I seek. I have weaved many examples of this through the stories in this book.

But I want to be clear. Awareness of my thoughts is an all-day and every day exercise. It is always at the forefront of my mind as I go through my day.

My father often told me, "Don't get stuck in short-term thinking that puts you in the scarcity trap." In other words, you don't need to deny outside circumstances or pretend they don't exist, but you also don't need to spend all your time thinking about them. Instead, activate some of your creative mental faculties (perception, will, reason, imagination, memory, and intuition) and do something constructive.

This way of thinking has helped guide how I think and what I choose to give energy to.

Over time I have created a paradigm of being deliberate with my days. I choose the thoughts I dismiss, and I choose the thoughts I give focus and emotion to.

As explained in the movie *The Secret*, we are magnets, and what we give energy to, we will attract. So why not give your energy to what you want?

When we listen to people around us, we may notice they focus on their worries or things they can do nothing about. This is often a waste of energy. What is needed is a simple redirect.

Don't get me wrong, you can't simply wish for a thing and have it appear. In fact, the Law of Attraction is secondary to the Law of Vibration, which is the primary law, and states that everything in our universe vibrates; nothing rests. Therefore, every single thing we want is already here. We don't have to get anything. Our job is to raise our awareness to be a vibrational match for the things we want. And the way to do this is to stay aware of our thoughts, constantly harvesting the good in order to reach higher levels.

I recently read a quote that explains this simply: "Everything is energy and that's all there is to it. Match the frequency of the reality you want, and you cannot help but get that reality." You need to get out and do the work to make it happen, but by giving it energy, you will find that you are more likely to do what is required to bring it into your life. Keep in mind that this works both ways. So, pay attention and make certain that your energy is not going to what you don't want.

Think about someone who is always positive and friendly. Typically, these people attract positivity into their lives. They see more opportunities each day and are often more productive. They are more likely to have successful businesses because people want to deal with them. They attract what they put out on a vibrational level.

On the flip side, we all know people who only seem to see the negative. As a result, they typically attract more negativity into their lives. Happiness and contentment always seem out of reach.

Have you noticed you don't want to be around someone like that? It is because they put out and attract negative energy (vibration) and tend to attract negative people. It is a self-fulfilling cycle; like attracts like.

Commit to the idea that you will consciously choose what you think about. The more you can maintain an awareness of your thoughts throughout your day, the more control you have over what comes into your life and also how you respond to what comes into your life.

Working toward a worthy goal is an excellent way to stay on track with your thoughts. In addition, it is a perfect way to keep aware of the vibration you are in.

I cannot remember a time that my Dad did not have a goal card in his pocket. And you did not want to be the one in the room without one when he started asking where yours was. This seemingly simple tool has been like a compass my entire life, and like my Dad, I always have one in my pocket.

If we don't have a goal, we work without direction, making us more susceptible to what is happening around us. It takes the strength of a worthy goal that we can feel on an emotional level to keep what is happening outside of us from affecting us.

I've found that I can better control my thoughts when I'm working towards something. The goal keeps me from simply bouncing along from day to day without direction. With a goal guiding me, I have order, and I stay focused on my destination. I don't worry about my next steps because they always reveal themselves along the way.

CONSIDER...

Design your life by choice, not chance. Commit to the idea that you will choose what you think about.

Controlling our thoughts in today's 24-hour news cycle can be more challenging than ever. And, let's face it, most of the news is negative. So, it is our job to ensure we are not falling prey to fear generated by that negativity.

Taking responsibility is a big step.

Notice if you are blaming outside circumstances or other people when things don't go right for you.

Create an affirmation.

Use this one or build one that resonates with you. For example, "I am the one who controls my thoughts and what I choose to think about."

What is your goal?
Goals can be both personal and professional.

Your goal should be something you think about multiple times a day; An image you've created and can go to quickly in your mind. You can feel what it feels like to have achieved it. You can see the colors and smell the smells; this is what it means to get emotionally involved with your goal.

NOTES:

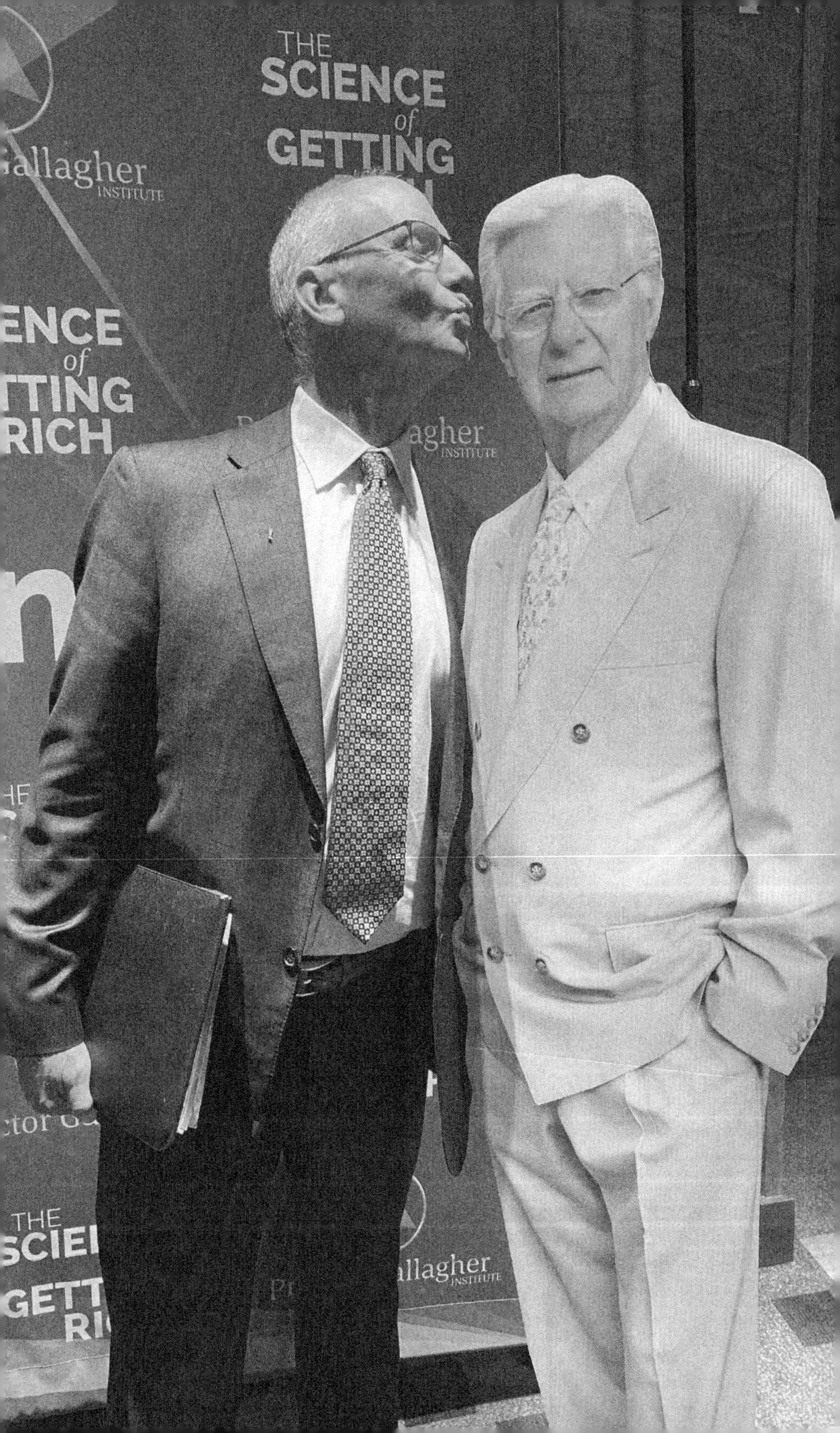
THE
SCIENCE
of
GETTING
INSTITUTE
RICH

CHAPTER 3

GRATITUDE

A Grateful Heart

" Gratitude is an attitude that hooks us up to our source of supply. And the more grateful you are, the closer you become to your maker, the architect of the universe, and the spiritual core of your being."
— Bob Proctor

While preparing for this chapter, I took out many of my old gratitude journals and read through them. A consistent theme throughout has been gratitude for my father. Remembering that I have always felt this way about my Dad does not surprise me but instead drives home how fortunate I have been to have lived this life with Bob Proctor as my father.

As I think of gratitude, I am transported to Dad's backyard. We have sat there together thousands of times. This was a special place for us. He loved the trees and small animals, especially the birds. We could sit quietly for hours, and sometimes he would say, "Listen to that!" 'That' was the sound of peace. I remember how grounded I felt being there with him.

Gratitude was a consistent theme in those quiet moments. Our conversations often went to how grateful he was for his life – for all there is and all there isn't. He truly lived his life with a grateful heart.

Continuously operating from a place of gratitude is how I was taught to show up, and I like that about myself. I live a better and more peaceful life because of it. Living with a grateful heart helps me create calm in my mind, and body, and ultimately, my world.

It is easy to be grateful when things are going well. However, my biggest breakthroughs and growth have often come after extreme challenges. Finding a way to be grateful while experiencing difficult times can help us to move through those times more quickly than if we just lived through it without the mindfulness of the good that is and the good that can come out of it.

Recognizing that there is good in everything instead of labeling feelings and situations as good or bad helps us to live in alignment with universal laws.

Over time, when you appreciate all there is, you will shift your outlook. A daily practice of gratitude helps you to reach a depth within that brings deep meaning to your life. As a result, you will feel empowered and inspired. You will feel in control of your thoughts and emotions, and you will operate with a sense of calm.

Your choices, not your circumstances, will create the life you desire.

I learned a strategy from my Dad at a very young age that I still use today. It's really effective at focusing my energy on my goals. When I sit to write in my gratitude journal each morning, I include how thankful I am for my life and the people in it. I then write things I am grateful for before they happen. Writing out that I am grateful for receiving, completing, or accomplishing something creates an expectation that what I want is already here. It creates an energy that puts me in the right vibration to receive.

A great example of this approach is the book you are now reading. Gratitude for this book appeared in my daily journal long before its physical form. Every day I would write how grateful I am that; "This book is read worldwide and well received." I also wrote, "I am grateful that the wisdom of my father that I have shared in these pages is helping others to live with a greater awareness of their potential." This last piece was necessary because of the emotional feeling it gave me to be helping people. To pass along a gift my father gave me for a lifetime means more than I can say.

Writing that statement didn't just attract the book to me. I also had to get on with the work, be persistent, and put in the effort. However, writing the statement put me in a grateful frame of mind and created the vision of what I wanted. It kept me focused on the bigger purpose of writing. Being thankful for it allowed me to open myself up to what would be and how good that would feel. It activated a great vibration, and when we work from this positive place on the energetic scale, "effort" is accompanied with ease – and work becomes a breeze.

Exercising gratitude can be immensely beneficial both psychologically and physically. Science has shown, an active gratitude practice can reduce the activation of fear and anxiety circuits in the brain and body and improve mood, focus, and sleep. In addition, it will open your heart and mind to the abundance surrounding you.

Though unseen with your eyes or other senses, gratitude quite literally creates connections in your Universe, much like a wireless connection between two devices can't be seen – regardless, the communication is there.

The thought pattern that a daily gratitude exercise sets up brings joy to each day and clears the way to see how everything is an opportunity to give thanks. Everything is an opportunity to grow, and everything is affected by how we think and feel about our life.

I like how Wallace Wattles puts it in his book *The Science of Getting Rich*. He said, "The grateful mind is constantly fixed upon the best. Therefore, it tends to become the best; it takes the form or character of the best and will receive the best."

I often share the stage with a good friend, Peggy McColl. Together we guide the audience through an exercise. It has become a fun part of what we do on stage together.

We ask the audience to write a letter to their future self – dated one year from the day they are writing it. After the letters are written, we have everyone put their name and address on their envelope and seal their letter. I keep these for one year and then mail them out. I'll never forget the first time I saw my letter arrive in my mailbox. Even knowing how powerful this exercise is, it was shocking to see how many of the things I had written a year earlier had manifested in my life.

You may have other ideas about living with a grateful heart. Do whatever feels right, but do something. How you do it is not nearly as important as doing it – don't get stuck in the details of 'how.'

Living in gratitude will change the way you see everything around you. It will change each day, and it will change how your life takes shape.

View from our waterfront home;
Attracted using the "future self letter" method.

CONSIDER...

**Take a moment now and think about what you are
grateful for. Close your eyes and <u>feel</u> it in your heart.**

*Can you feel the shift? When I do this, I feel my heart expand. I do this
exercise many times throughout the day. It doesn't take long and makes a big
difference, not just in the moment but in shaping my future.*

Write a letter to your future self.

1. *Begin by closing your eyes and visualizing what your life
   will look like in one year. Imagine everything has worked
   out even better than you'd imagined.*

2. *Imagine how you will feel. Then, start writing,
   congratulating yourself for all you have accomplished.*

3. *Write it from the perspective of having already
   accomplished your heart's desires.*

4. *Use emotional words that touch your heart and are
   meaningful to you.*

5. *Make it fun.*

This is an excellent exercise for living into your future.

When doing this, take the lid off your imagination and write some things you want but have no idea how you will accomplish. The important thing is to get creative and have fun.

The exercise may seem silly, but it is powerful. This is also a fantastic exercise to do with children. Have them imagine what they want to accomplish over the next year and help them articulate and write it down.

After you seal your letter in an envelope, date it a year from now and store it in your desk calendar or planner. When the date arrives to open your letter, notice the feelings you experience while reading it. After you have finished reading it, a good practice is to immediately write yourself another letter for the following year.

The world ebbs and flows – and gratitude should be a state of mind; an attitude to live by regardless of our day-to-day circumstances. What may feel like the worst thing today could actually end up being the best thing. Trust the process. Remember: Things are always working out for you!

Get a journal or notebook and dedicate it to your daily gratitude practice. Make this practice non-negotiable by committing to do it every day — regardless.

NOTES:

CHAPTER 4

COMMUNICATE YOUR FEELINGS

Father's Day

"Dad, you've always been my hero."
— Brian Procter

My father was born during the great depression, and soon after, his father was sent to Europe to fight in World War II. When his father returned, he was not the same man. Like many men of that time, his wounds were deep. I don't know much about my grandfather; it was not something Dad spoke about. If it came up, he would say, "It is what it is," and then he would turn the conversation to his beautiful life and what a wonderful mother he had.

I always marveled at what a good father Dad was despite not having that as a young boy. He would often say that his life was magnificent and that riches take many forms, and one of the things he enjoyed most was his family.

He passed that love of parenting on to me. Dad was an excellent example for me to model. He supported and encouraged me; most importantly, he was always there for me. That never wavered. I knew I could call him at any time, and he would pick up the phone and be happy to talk with me.

Around 1980, my mother was planning to get married again; and my father moved back to Canada from the United States with his love interest, Linda (who later became his wife) so that he could live with us full-time.

Linda is eighteen years younger than my father, so when she moved with him to Canada, she was only twenty-seven. Unfortunately, at that young age, Linda had already been tragically widowed when her first husband died from an unexpected but long illness; because of his condition, Linda and her husband had not had the opportunity to have children together. That means that when Linda moved to Canada with Dad, she was agreeing to not only move to a new country; she was also stepping into a ready-made and active family with three teenagers: 18, 16, and 14.

Dad and Linda together showed us love in a way that felt selfless and complete. They taught us the importance of priorities and values.

Dad had to rebuild his business from scratch in Canada. However, this time he wanted to create a new model where he was not traveling and leaving us at home. This decision meant building a professional reputation that was local. That was not an easy choice financially, but he was willing to do whatever it took so that we could all be together.

He and Linda went on to get married and were married for close to 40 years when he passed. Dad dedicated his book, *You Were Born Rich*, to Linda. He wrote, "Dedicated to Linda who brought the sun from the south and willingly shared it with Brian, Colleen and Raymond." As you can imagine, we are all very grateful to Linda and love her dearly.

When I was fortunate enough to be near my father on Father's Day, we would have a BBQ with the entire family in his backyard. His backyard was his sanctuary. It is where he preferred to be, and my memories of those times are vivid. I can close my eyes and see his smile as he looks around at all of us, his kids, grandkids, and great-grandkids.

If I was not near him on this day, Dad and I would instead have a long phone conversation and reminisce. There was always a lot of laughing. My father had the best laugh. You couldn't hear it without smiling; it was that kind of laugh. It turned heads.

Today, as I write this it is Father's Day and what I am most thankful for is that we were both able to say everything we needed and wanted to say to each other before he passed on. So many people don't get that chance, and I know what a gift that was.

I can still hear the things he said to me from his hospital bed and the tender and loving way he spoke; he was so kind. He knew his time was limited, and he wanted to make sure every person in his family understood his love for them.

Often while in the hospital, when he would drift off to sleep while I was next to him, I would type into my phone what he had said to me so that I would not forget a single word. I go back to those notes often and feel his love.

We put my father's urn into his final resting place only a week ago. It was a beautiful day. The birds were singing, and the entire family was there. We all felt wrapped in Dad's love for us and also our love for each other.

We each took a few minutes to share a memory of something Dad taught us. It was bittersweet to be saying our final goodbye in this way. But to feel his love like a warm hug around us – all together - would have been exactly what he'd wanted.

When it was my turn to speak, I had one thought repeating in my mind: I knew it was Dad talking to me. He wanted me to make sure that his family felt his love. So, I spoke about the different ways Dad made time for each of us and how he loved us uniquely as individuals; how he taught us to love our children, friends, and family in deep and meaningful ways.

At this moment, I also shared something that made everyone laugh but drove home the point of Dad's fierce desire to make us feel special.

I talked about a time in the hospital just before he passed. I had been with him for several hours, and it was late into the night. As I was getting up to leave, he pulled me in close. I was surprised by his strength and urgency. I thought he was going to say something. But instead, he moved my face mask down and pulled me in for a big kiss on the lips. He then looked deep into my eyes and told me how much he loved me.

I remember walking out of the hospital vibrating and with tears in my eyes.

My father was a strong and unique man. I am hard-pressed to recall a time as an adult when my Dad kissed me on my lips. It caught me by surprise; the intimacy of the act felt like an exchange of energy. I could feel the power that still lived within him.

CONSIDER...

*Do the people you are close to in your life
know how much you love them?*

Leave no doubt in the mind of your loved ones. Please do it now. Let them know right away. I know my father left us with peace in his heart because this is how he lived his life. It is an example I encourage you to follow.

NOTES:

"The blame game is a dumb game."
– Bob Proctor

CHAPTER 5

FORGIVENESS

Finding Freedom

"True forgiveness means that we choose to accept things as they are, extract the good, and let go of the rest."
— Bob Proctor

I had just hung up the phone following a heartfelt discussion with my father. It was as I was writing this chapter. I called him because I had a question about his thoughts on forgiveness. You see, I have witnessed him reclaim his inner peace following a betrayal or hurt many times throughout my life.

Over the years, I heard Dad share stories about people who had taken advantage of him. But he never seemed to harbor any negative thoughts about the other person.

He explained to me that he is so practiced at guarding his mind against thoughts that don't serve him that he doesn't give his betrayers any thought at all. He doesn't let them enter his mind.

And if they do, he immediately replaces that thought with something else or picks up one of his dogs to change his focus. He will never do business with or engage with them again; however, he will not allow the experience or person to cast a cloud on his life. Instead, he literally releases the person to their highest good and him to his.

He then said something I have heard him say many times when teaching. "Holding a negative thought of someone in your mind only damages you. Forgiveness is for you, not the other person. Most people think that if John hurts me and I forgive him, I do it for John's benefit. I'm not; it is for my benefit. I am the one releasing what is bothering me. By taking responsibility for my peace of mind, I choose how to respond to it."

I looked up the definition of Forgiveness:

> *Psychologists generally define Forgiveness as a conscious, deliberate decision to release feelings of resentment or vengeance toward a person or group who has harmed you. Regardless of whether they deserve your Forgiveness. Forgiveness does not mean forgetting, nor does it mean condoning or excusing offenses.*

That definition supports what my father taught me, allowing me to see that forgiveness is about how those feelings affect me.

I have chosen to make forgiveness an adventure. For me, the word adventure has a positive connotation that relates to experience and growth.

Several years ago, someone I was close to did things that caused me extreme mental and emotional pain. I can still remember the way my entire body felt. It was a deep hurt that I felt on a visceral level, and I never wanted to experience again. It was a situation that took me a lot of time and courage to forgive.

Unfortunately, I continued that relationship for an additional two years after learning what she had said and done. I did this because I wanted to ensure I had tried everything possible to make it work.

When I look back on it, the real reason I stayed so long is that I feared I would look weak to my friends and family. As a middle-aged man, I had yet to have great success in romantic relationships. "What would everyone think of me failing again?"

I was wrong for staying and not leaving. By caring what others would think of me, I created more pain and resentment for myself. It wasn't healthy.

To move on and release myself from the discomfort of it all, I knew I had to face how I got there, and I needed to forgive her completely. I also needed to forgive myself. I was punishing myself for letting it drag on the way I had and for staying in a place that did not honor me or my principles.

This last relationship betrayal convinced me I would never settle again. I had said this before, but this time was different.

I remember Dad saying to me, "You can't change the time you got out of bed this morning." I love that – such a simple reminder to look forward, not backward. What has happened in the past has happened. And now it is just that, a part of the past.

So how can you forgive someone, or even yourself, and make it an 'adventure' – an experience you learn from? I did it by opening my heart and working to direct my thoughts from a place of empathy, gentleness, and kindness. The release I felt was gradual initially, but I could stay with my thoughts longer with time. Soon I could feel freedom in my entire being.

With love for myself, I gave myself permission to let go. Letting go is not forgetting; it is dulling pain's sharp edges and replacing that with self-love. And to love yourself, you must learn to let go. By letting go, I weakened the turmoil my body was experiencing from my thoughts. Finally, I began to feel more free mentally, emotionally, and physically. I could exhale.

In Bob Proctor's seminars and programs, Dad encouraged people to send love to those that have caused them pain — it's the person that causes your chest to tighten, and maybe your stomach hurts when you think about them. This person can even be you. This exercise creates peace and harmony within and, with consistent practice, brings freedom from anger and hurt. It is to make space to allow good to come into our lives.

Do this exercise in a quiet room – close your eyes and imagine the person causing you pain. Next, fill your heart, mind, and body with warm energy. You may even find yourself becoming emotional during this exercise. That is good!

Is this an easy thing to do? Maybe not. But personal growth is a choice, and forgiveness gives you freedom. You can choose to grow and be free. By forgiving, you are freeing yourself to move on and experience better in your life by removing the blockage that anger and hurt create.

CONSIDER...

Is an experience, person, or memory causing you pain?

We can't change what has happened, and we cannot change what is outside of us. The only thing we can change is what we do with it. We can change our framing of how we think and feel about it.

When you notice the ruminating thoughts of the experience, person, or memory that caused you pain, take a deep breath and ask yourself, "Is this thought empowering me or draining me?"

You do not need to be a victim in your story. Being a victim is very different from being victimized.

Do less blaming and use your awareness to recognize when you are in the blaming loop. This includes self-blame, which is the ultimate form of emotional abuse.

Do you make life choices based on what others will think of you?

Worrying about approval from others is 'the fear of being found out,' or 'the fear of looking bad.' It's that negative loop of telling yourself that you are an imposter. It comes from doubting yourself.

You need to face that fear and let go of the need for other people's approval. When you do this, you will discover your authentic self.

When you find the part of you that doesn't care what others think, you will more easily build meaningful relationships. This is because you will be lining up your actions, thoughts, and behaviors with your core values.

What would happen if you loosened your grip on thoughts that hijack your mind?

Always remember that you control the script, and you can shape that script. What would happen next in your life if you just dropped your end of the rope of whatever struggle you are dealing with and freed up your resources to engage in building positive, productive behaviors?

NOTES:

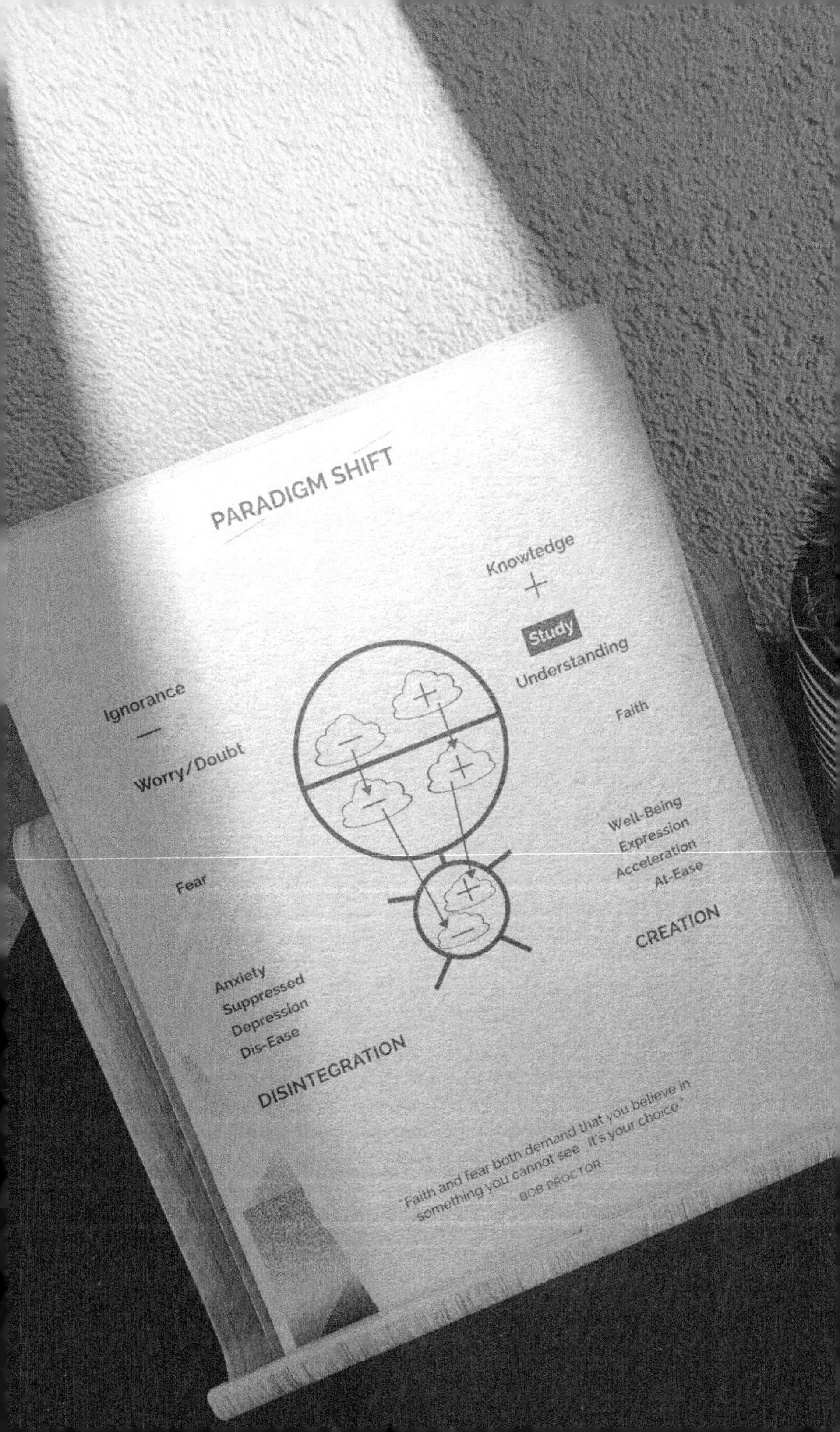

PARADIGM SHIFT

Knowledge

$+$

Study

Understanding

Ignorance

—

Worry/Doubt

Faith

Fear

Well-Being
Expression
Acceleration
At-Ease

CREATION

Anxiety
Suppressed
Depression
Dis-Ease

DISINTEGRATION

"Faith and fear both demand that you believe in
something you cannot see. It's your choice."
— BOB PROCTOR

CHAPTER 6

DECISION

How Do You See It?

*"Faith and fear both demand that you
believe in something you cannot see.
You choose!"*
— Bob Proctor

When my father spoke about using your mental faculty of perception, he would drive home the point that our choices, not circumstances, create the life we desire. What is significant to one person may be small to another, and in our effort to grow and learn, we must be willing to use perception to consider the many sides of a person, situation, or circumstance.

It was always fun to watch the confusion unfold in the room when Dad would hold up a book and ask the audience if they saw the front or back. Of course, they would say they saw the front. Dad insisted it was the back, which would turn into a scenario of 'who's right?' Finally, he would point out that they were all right.

The audience could see the front, but my father, holding the book up, could see only the back.

Many years ago, Dad reminded me of this lesson in perception when I was looking to purchase a home in Florida. I had fallen in love with a house that I felt was out of my price range. I spoke to him about the house and the price, saying I thought the cost was prohibitive. He paused, looked me in the eyes, and asked, "Compared to what?" When I continued to argue my point by telling him the asking price, he responded, "That's all?"

With those words, he caused me to change my perception instantly, which changed my perspective. It was as if the clouds in my mind parted.

My relationship with my Dad has taught me that sometimes you must borrow someone else's belief in you when your belief in yourself is not on solid ground. Having Bob Proctor believe in me has kept me going when I couldn't see how I would get there or find the strength.

Throughout my adult life, there have been times when Dad and I have lived far from each other. But, during those years, we always found ways to spend time together. One year, he and Linda rented a home in Florida close to where I was living. So, having him close gave us a lot of quiet, quality time together.

During his time in Florida that year, I knew I needed his belief in me. Again, I was struggling with a decision about a house that would take me way out of my comfort zone. I knew in my heart that I wanted to go for it, but I was scared. I needed that extra push.

No one pushes you like Bob Proctor. I know from experience that if I ask my father if he thinks I should do something out of my comfort zone, I am setting myself up to go for it. So, I told Dad I needed some advice and asked to have lunch with him to discuss it.

I let my thoughts flow as we sat outside in the beautiful Florida sunshine. He listened patiently as I explained the second home Cory and I had purchased on the water at the southern end of Puget Sound in Washington State. The location is gorgeous, with an expansive view. However, although patched together over the years, the original house had been built in 1903 and needed a lot of work. Essentially, the home was a teardown, but we would have to call it a remodel because its original build location was so near the water; it is much closer to the water than a home would be allowed to be built today. There were various permits, government agency surveys, and – of course – significant costs that would be involved.

It felt extremely complicated and costly because we also wanted to accomplish all of this without seeking a loan to pay for it. This would require a large sum of money over the next year or so; money we did not have. Sure, we had some of it, but nowhere near what we needed to complete the project in cash, and once we signed the contract, we were committed.

While explaining this, I went over all the different ideas Cory and I had brainstormed to make it happen.

Now here is the thing. Although I was struggling with the decision, I knew how much I wanted it, so I was ultimately aligned with my desire. My heart was going full-speed ahead, but my head was trying to slow me down... I was scared.

But as I've said, I would not have asked Bob Proctor – my father – for advice if I didn't want to do it. I was putting myself on the hook by talking with him.

As I continued telling him how we could bring in income, I felt excited. Finally, Dad stopped me and said, "Brian, do you really want this? You will find a way to make this happen if your want is strong enough. You do not need to figure it all out right here, right now. If this idea scares you, then you are likely on the right track."

While sitting there and hearing myself talk, I knew I had committed to moving forward. I quickly went from a desire to a decision to a committed decision. That is part of the wonder of being in Bob Proctor's energy; anything feels possible, and you will frequently find yourself experiencing quantum leaps.

I left that lunch knowing I wasn't looking back. So, each day I wrote out – and thought about – this goal. I added detail to my vision of this house completed. Cory and I would talk about it each night at dinner. We would get excited and talk about having the kids together at the house and what that would feel like. The energy we were putting into this added to the realness of the goal completed. Each day, I became clearer on what needed to be done to achieve it. I was paying attention to daily opportunities and taking action.

It wasn't long before I became obsessed! And obsessed is what you need to be. You need to fuse with your desire. Dad had been teaching me this lesson for as long as I can remember, and it makes me laugh to think of his patience as he listened to me at the age of 57, asking him if he thought I should go for it.

Today as I write these words, Cory and I are living in that beautiful custom-built home on the water and loving every minute of it. And we are also proud of everything we did to get here.

By only focusing on how we could do it, we no longer gave any energy to why we couldn't. As a result, in a relatively short period, we were able to build the house we truly wanted – the way we wanted.

At our Matrixx events that were held in Toronto, we worked closely with each client to coach them on the initial stages of goal setting and help them stretch to their BIG C-type goal, a goal that excites and scares them at the same time. During the first part, we would work on their vision and help them to create an emotional attachment to that vision with descriptive words that excited them. Then, we would coach them on staying open to questioning their beliefs about accomplishing big goals. Finally, we would guide them to stay out of the idea of HOW at this stage. That is precisely what Dad did with me that day in Florida. Once he got me on track – nothing stopped me.

Now when I am working on something I know will cause me to stretch, I tap into that memory of sitting with him at that restaurant in Florida. By stepping back and altering my perception, I can create multiple perspectives that change everything. My most significant growth has happened when I have been my most uncomfortable.

There is a quote by Steve Jobs that Dad liked to use:

> *"You can't connect the dots looking forward; you can only connect them looking backward. So, you must trust that the dots will somehow connect in your future. You must trust in something – your gut, destiny, life, karma, whatever. This approach has never let me down and has made all the difference in my life."*

What Steve Jobs said makes so much sense to me. I could never have imagined what obstacles I would face when working to achieve some of my biggest goals, let alone plan for them; knowing the specifics of challenges in advance may have held me back. That is why faith in what you want and your ability to achieve it is essential. I have gotten to where I get excited about the feeling of fear because I know it means growth. As Bob Proctor said, "Stop overthinking; it's ok not to know the answers. Answers will come to you when you least expect them. Relax."

CONSIDER...

Do you have a desire that you push aside because you cannot imagine how you would achieve it?

Everything is possible. It doesn't matter if you are starting small or that it may be a while before you get there – your growth occurs in the process of the journey.

Stay open to the fact that anything is possible for you. Believing in yourself and surrounding yourself with others who believe in you will bring more of yourself to the surface.

And when you get there, you will have created something even more beautiful than you originally imagined.

What does it mean to change your perception?

Maintaining a singular perception in your life can prohibit your growth. Think about how frequently we get locked into our point of view as the right way, the only way, or the best way. Instead, consider that there could very well be a better way – different from the one you see right now.

Remaining open to the certainty that everything is perception widens your view. I am so conscious of this when I talk to people; I never lock into my idea as the only way. Dad taught me to be open to the fundamental fact that everything has many sides.

NOTES:

Getting 'Unstuck'

"You are the only problem you will ever have, and you are the only solution."
— Bob Proctor

Recognize that everything is temporary, including feeling stuck.

If you are not where you want to be in life, it is you that must decide to do something about it. Nothing is achieved without effort. And the best part is that when you decide and start taking action, it won't be long before you begin to see things differently. Making the decision is the hard part. Once that is done, your mind will become laser-focused, and you will make moves with intention.

Sometimes during a seminar, we would bring in guests and entertainment. One time, in Los Angeles, we brought in comedian and transformational speaker Kyle Cease. Kyle said something from the stage that stuck with all of us: "When wrestling with a decision, you can only measure what you are giving up; you cannot measure what you will gain."

Unfortunately, that 'unknown' is what keeps us stuck where we are, even if we are unhappy. Staying stuck means we know what to expect... so we stay there because change can feel scary, and we cannot measure the gain of what that change could bring.

Whenever I was struggling, Dad would start asking me questions. "Brian, what are your limiting beliefs about this? Why are you holding on to those beliefs, and what can you do to change them?"

Those questions would get me thinking. Dad knew that he needed to get me to examine my thinking and that if he could push me to face what was holding me back, I would be able to do the work to make a change that was necessary for me to reach my next level.

One of these conversations with my father happened because of the resistance I felt about getting on stage at our events. I knew I had a message I could share, but I always got so nervous before I went up that I often felt that the message I was sharing was unclear due to my nervousness.

Each morning while on the road for an event and before the day got rolling, Dad and I would enjoy an early morning cup of coffee together in his hotel room. That was a special time for both of us. During one of those mornings, I brought up my anxiousness about going on stage that afternoon. I could feel myself stuck in a loop of fear.

Dad looked me in the eyes and said two things to me that made all the difference. "First and foremost," he said, "It is none of your business what those people think of you." I have heard him say that many times in many situations, but applying it to myself in that scenario gave it new meaning. However, it was the next thing he said that got me unstuck. He said, "If you are nervous on stage, the mistake you are making is that you're thinking about yourself rather than the value of what you have to share with the audience. Everything will change if you take the focus off of yourself and instead focus on serving."

He coached me to engage with the group as if I was having a relaxed conversation with a friend. Then, he said, "Brian, you have no idea how what you have to share could impact even one person. That is why we are here. That is why we share our knowledge and experiences. It is why we share our stories. It is so others can gain. Focus outward and focus on adding value."

That conversation got me – unstuck. I have never been afraid again when speaking in front of an audience. If I ever hesitate, I take a deep breath, narrow my focus to the people in front of me and think back to that conversation with Dad in his hotel room, and then I speak from my heart.

An exercise that has helped me when I feel anxious is to bring myself fully into the present moment. Our mind causes all our suffering. When stressed or anxious, we are either living in the past or building a picture of a dire future. I have trained myself to shift my thoughts with intention to what I can do right here, right now, to make this moment better. I ask myself, "How can I contribute?" Then I push myself to participate, and to show up.

Get excited about what is next for you, and be excited about today. These actions will help to get you unstuck.

CONSIDER...

How do you weaken limiting beliefs?

You replace them with a new belief.

Most of the time, we are unaware of our limiting beliefs. We don't even consider that our thoughts and beliefs could be what are holding us back.

So, to create meaningful change, we must examine our beliefs – on money, love, relationships, work, business, etc. – and we need to examine them often.

As you gain an understanding of what they are, write them out. Then begin doing the work to alter those limitations by directing your thoughts to create something different. Write their polar opposite!

Doing this work could change a pattern that has existed for generations within your family. You can end those patterns by changing a belief that is possibly holding you and others back.

It's also important to figure out what old wounds you are hanging on to and why you're holding on to them. What triggers those memories? Those wounds can become a part of our belief system, and hanging onto them could be a coping mechanism to avoid being accountable for current circumstances.

When you shine a light on that realization, you can begin the work of healing.

Try this exercise.

Close your eyes and think about what you really want. How does that make you feel? Can you see yourself receiving it, or does a limiting belief start to show itself?

In these moments of looking at what you want, identify your limiting beliefs by paying attention to thoughts that interfere with your desire. It will appear as an, "I can't do that because..." or "Who do you think you are that you could be, do, or have that?"

Don't beat yourself up for having those thoughts or if those thoughts return. You're not responsible for the limiting beliefs you've acquired before today. However, you are responsible now for changing them.

So instead of being frustrated with yourself, simply stand in awareness and focus on replacing them with thoughts that support your desire. Focus on strengthening your mind by being prepared with supportive self-affirmations when limiting thoughts arise.

Change your channel and make the new channel stronger by spending more time there. Give your new channel (new way of thinking) the loudest voice in your head.

NOTES:

Dad and me during a visit to Florida

CHAPTER 7

MAKING AN IMPRESSION

Creating Paradigms That Stick

"We come this way but once.
We can either tiptoe through life and hope
that we get to death without being too badly bruised,
or we can live a full life achieving our goals and
realizing our wildest dreams."
— Bob Proctor

As I mentioned earlier, when someone learns that Bob Proctor is my father, they typically ask, "What's it like to be Bob Proctor's son?" The following story is a glimpse of my answer from my viewpoint as a young child.

I often share this story because of its incredible impact on me as a young boy and how the memory still affects me today. It is the story of a simple act – a bedtime ritual Dad created.

Every night when Dad was not traveling, he would be the one who tucked me into bed. When he did this, he had a particular way of ending my day, a practice that ensured that I would feel special, loved, seen, and heard when I closed my eyes at night.

He would sit on the edge of the bed and put his hand on my chest. Then he would softly speak encouraging words about what a great life I lived and what a great person I was. He would say things that showed me that he saw who I was and how I treated myself and others. Sometimes, he would reinforce something that he observed in me or something happening in my life at the time and help me see the good in it, even if it was something that I thought was bad. He taught me at that young age that there is good in everything.

He was helping me to choose beliefs and showing me how to align them with habits that would serve me. And through this exercise, he was teaching me to plant ideas into my subconscious mind.

Dad would genuinely listen when I spoke, always being patient. I realize now that with this practice, he made me feel comfortable and loved so I could let myself be vulnerable with sharing my thoughts. He also taught me how to reflect and examine; to question and identify gaps between what I was saying and my behavior.

When he did this, he always spoke gently and with his hand on my chest to keep physical contact as we spoke.

Then, just before leaving the room and saying goodnight, he would say, "Brian, you are capable of being, doing, or having anything that you desire. When you wake up in the morning, you will feel wonderful and have a big smile on your face."

I continued this bedtime practice with my children when they were young. I called it a "Dream Pact." It was a way to imprint positive statements and mirror beliefs or behaviors that would help them grow into confident and healthy adults.

At bedtime, I would sit with my kids and create stories with positive images where they were the hero. I would weave messages of strength into their heart and mind to instill in them that they were in charge and controlled their lives. We would also talk about their day and I would point out all the good and show them how they made a difference. These ideas would help them fall asleep feeling confident, capable, and smiling.

My relationship with my children has always been loving and honest. In my mind, we seldom had trying times. They have always been self-aware, loving people, and I am proud of them.

Growing up with Bob Proctor as my father and mentor set the stage for that. This bedtime ritual he created would be an excellent example of environmental conditioning that has now been passed down as a positive paradigm to three generations.

Dad's example helped me to raise the next generation with love,

Four generations of Proctors

kindness, and understanding. And now, as my children start their own families, I watch how they treat their kids. I know Dad did not grow up with this in his life as a young boy, but in creating this exercise, he established the foundation of love and trust that has bonded three – and now, four – generations together, and it all started with what I'm sure he saw as a simple act of kindness.

The most minor things in life can often be the most meaningful and can become the greatest source of happiness throughout our entire lives.

This practice my father created is such a part of my subconscious that even now, decades later, when I lay down to sleep, I can feel his hand on my chest, guiding me to be, do and have whatever my heart desires. The memory instantly puts me in a place of gratitude.

I love this quote from Maya Angelou and think of it often when talking to people. It reminds me to conduct myself in a way that I will be a person who is remembered for making others feel good.

"I've learned that people will forget what you said, people will forget what you did, but people will never forget how you made them feel." – Maya Angelou

And it is never too late to be that person. It always begins with ourselves.

CONSIDER...

What sort of behavior do you model to those close to you and to the world?

If you are a parent, consider what you teach your children through your words, feelings, thoughts, and, ultimately, your actions. We know kids learn from what they see, experience and feel. And the memories that take root when we are young are strong. They are the ones we don't forget, and they either support us or we spend our lives trying to forget them in order to reshape our future. But whether we like it or not, they do create a foundation.

Every day is a new opportunity.

You have an opportunity right now to create generational change for the better by establishing new paradigms that will be passed down. Paradigms that result in confidence and feelings of self-worth. Whether your children are still young or already adults, it's never too late to step into your power to influence.

NOTES:

Family road trip; 1977

Road Trips

*"The real joy in life is
the day-to-day experiences."*
- Bob Proctor

In 1976, Cadillac was producing its last convertible. It was a beautiful, heart-stopping Eldorado, and Bob Proctor wanted that car. Dad talked endlessly about how it would feel to drive it with the top down and how he could see himself in the driver's seat.

I vividly remember the day he drove that car into our driveway. The car seemed to glide with its shiny white exterior and tan, ultra-soft leather interior. It was enormous, even for the days of the giant gas guzzlers; this model seemed to command space around it. To my young eyes, it seemed to take up our entire driveway.

This memory of my father bringing home that car is easy for me to recall when I close my eyes; I can feel how the sun felt that day, and I can vividly see the pride and joy that was emanating from Dad as he explained the features and fine details to us kids. Even the neighbors slowed to look when they walked by. To us, the car looked and felt magical.

There is a picture on the wall downstairs at my father's home. It is a family photo taken somewhere in the middle of the desert in the southwest part of the United States. You can see the wind blowing and the harshness of the environment in our hair. The picture is from a road trip in that car, of a special time that left a significant impression on my young heart and soul.

It was not long after Dad got that car that he took my siblings and me on that cross-country road trip where that picture was taken. We drove from Toronto, Canada, to Los Angeles. It was the summer of 1977. I was 15, my sister Colleen was 13, and my brother Raymond was 11. It's a trip we still reminisce about today. It is also the trip where I learned what it meant to be living in the joy of the moment.

I'm not sure how many days that drive took, but I do remember the fun we had on this journey. This trip was about something other than getting to Los Angeles as fast as possible. It was about enjoying the drive and experiencing different things along the way. This trip became the metaphor in my life for enjoying the journey.

During this road trip, if any of us wanted to stop for any reason, we would stop. We stopped frequently and randomly as if we had all the time in the world, not in a hurry to get anywhere. We would pull over to try fishing in a river or look at an interesting rock formation. We would explore small towns or check out a local diner. We even attended a parade in Kansas that was re-enacting the outlaw Dalton Brothers Gang. We also stopped to see Arizona's Petrified Forest and Meteor Crater. I remember staying in a small motel just because they had a pool out front that we wanted to swim in.

As we drove across the desert with the rooftop down, wind whipping through our hair, what I remember most is the big belly laughter from all of us and the energy of joy that filled the car.

Dad was all about discovering. He taught us to have that same sense of curiosity and wonder and made us feel like our thoughts were valued by listening to and acting on our ideas. He made the time to include us in the decision-making of our journey, showing us our desires mattered.

Once I had kids, I would take them on weekend trips. I made sure they felt valued the same way by including them in the decision-making. I would let them pick the place, and we stayed open to the unexpected and possibilities. We would explore and discover together without an agenda, and, most importantly, we would spend time together.

This intentional way of being with Danny and Leanne was because of the effect that the vacations, short trips, and meetings out of town with my father had on me throughout my life.

To this day, my kids remember those adventures. Those times helped shape our relationships and played a part in who they are today. It will be fun for me to hear the stories they tell me about their kids and their memorable adventures together.

CONSIDER...

What does it mean to you to be in the moment?

Stay present – especially with your loved ones. Connect with other humans; pause and feel grateful for that connection.

Put away your cell phone and make eye contact. Enjoy face-to-face time with the people in your life. Ask how the other person is doing; listen, hug them, and be present.

Take care of yourself – you are worth it.

What can you do to build lasting connections?

Shared experiences and history built with intention is a big part of what brings people close, especially as time passes and our lives go in different directions. These shared experiences make us feel more connected.

Choose to add value to people's lives. It can be as simple as active listening.

Meaningful connection with others deepens our own sense of self-worth and purpose. What steps can you take to connect with someone today?

NOTES:

Dad with his beloved mother Marguerite

My Grandmother

"Mothers are the most important people in the world; they give us life. And for that alone, we should be grateful."
— Bob Proctor

For as long as I can remember, I watched Dad take care of his mother in a way that her needs and happiness lived at the forefront of his mind. He did whatever he could to improve her life, and he understood how important it was to spend time with her, not just for her but also for him.

Along with his siblings, Helen and Al, they would plan trips and outings that included her, which were sure to delight her. Watching how Dad cared for his mother and paying attention to how he spoke to and about her influenced how I came to treat my own mother and both my grandmothers.

It was at the age of 55 that my grandmother (known to all the grandkids and great-grandkids as Nan) decided to spend her winters in Florida. She bought a lovely home and would spend six months of the year there right up until the time she passed away in her nineties.

Dad was so happy to see her living the life she wanted. One year he bought her a car so she could get around and he could rest easy knowing she had something safe to drive in. When I was younger, he would send me to Florida to be with her for the drive back to Toronto. Those road trips with Nan are some of my favorite memories when I think of her today.

Nan was fun and curious like Dad, and she had a natural sense of wonder. She made friends wherever she went. Hooters was one of her favorite places to stop and eat during those drives between Florida and Toronto. She knew where every one of those restaurants was along the route. Learning this about Nan makes people laugh, but she loved the chicken wings; so much so that she could get a vegetarian excited about those wings with her passionate and descriptive details of the flavor and the happiness that eating them brought her.

Nan was born in the month of February, and every year Dad made it a point to make her birthday a big celebration. She was always in Florida that month, so that is where we celebrated. Dad made sure she had a party that included the many friends she had made there. And he always encouraged her to invite everyone, then he took care of all the details. Transportation, food, drink, entertainment – whatever was needed.

One year, Nan's list of guests was so extensive Dad had to change the venue and rent a bus. At this stage in life, Nan and her guests were well into their 80's. On this birthday, the bus took the group into Tampa to a nice restaurant for a private dinner. The liquor bill ended up being higher than the food bill. Linda remembers the bus being very rowdy on the way to the party and very quiet on the way back because all the guests were asleep. We still laugh about that birthday trip.

I don't ever remember seeing Nan without a smile on her face. She was a remarkable woman and deeply loved by her family.

My father didn't just treat Nan that way; he made sure all his family felt important. It could be as simple as a kind word or making time for a private conversation. He made certain that he was consistently available and generous; he regularly expressed gratitude to all of us that we were in his life. And because gratitude operates on a higher frequency than anger or disappointment, living the way Dad did created calm around him.

CONSIDER...

**Keep your promises and live generously –
with your time, energy, and money.**

Dad taught me that relationships are not perfect, but if you strive to be the best version of yourself, you will see and harvest the good of what is.

Go the extra step to mend and heal your relationships if that is what's needed.

Assume the best in those around you. Do this by checking in with your attitude. Suspend any negative thoughts or disbeliefs you have that are based on past experiences.

In the long run, you will be the benefactor of your efforts because how you treat others reflects how you feel inside. You will never regret being the one people respect and can count on. And you will never regret the freedom that comes from practicing non-judgement.

NOTES:

Clouds

"The magnificence of the mind is that it can tap into thought and create whatever image it chooses."
— Bob Proctor

When I was a young boy, Dad and I would lie on our backs out on the lawn and stare at the summer sky. I can still remember the feeling of the cool grass on my skin and the warm sun on my face. It was always when the sky was filled with white puffy clouds slowly floating by that Dad would say, "Let's go practice."

He would tell me, "Brian, pick a small cloud and let's make it disappear." At that age, I never questioned him and just went with it.

Once we had a small cloud picked out, he instructed me to focus all my attention on that cloud. Then, he told me to send warm energy and picture the cloud burning away into nothing. At first, I thought this was a little silly. But, that said, Dad's way of learning was infectious; you couldn't help but get caught up in his passion.

In no time at all, we were making small clouds disappear! The first time it happened, I thought it was just the winds making them go away, but as we kept picking other clouds and sending warm energy and focus, they were the only clouds fading away. We were really doing it. I remember telling the other kids at school about it, and they thought I was crazy. And that was okay.

Looking back on this, the entire experience was whimsical and enjoyable. Later in my life, I realized what my father had taught me. In a fun way, he cleared a path to show me how to focus my thoughts on one thing for an extended period of time. As a result, I learned at a young age about the power of concentration and strengthening my will, which has served me well all my life.

CONSIDER...

How is your power of concentration and focus? Can you hold one thought in your mind to the exclusion of all other distractions?

Holding more than one thought in your mind creates confusion, and giving your entire focus to a singular thought creates an energy that will grow that thought. You are now - and you will become - what you think about most often.

An exercise Dad gave that was meant to develop one's ability to focus was what he called the candle exercise. He would suggest placing a lit candle opposite your favorite chair. Next, turn off all lights and other distractions, including your phone, and focus all your attention on the flame. After a few seconds, your mind may start to wander. When you notice this happening, simply bring your mind and focus back to the flame. Don't worry about the fact that your mind is wandering. Instead, gently bring your attention back to the flame.

Focus is a necessary skillset for achievement. This exercise will help you strengthen your ability to concentrate on one thing at the exclusion of all others.

Where attention goes, energy is flowing. You are training yourself in the process of manifestation through focused intention.

NOTES:

CHAPTER 8

MINDSET

Purpose, Passion, and Persistence

*"The only limits in our life
are those we impose on ourselves."
— Bob Proctor*

Dad made it easy to be with him and experience how he earned a living.

I was always proud when watching him work with a small group or teach from the stage with thousands of people listening. Watching how he engaged with the audience, whether large or small and how the audience was hungry for the message he was sharing reinforced how fortunate I was to be his audience of one so often. I've had a front-row seat my entire life, seeing how Bob Proctor made a difference in this world.

During a breakfast we had together while in Los Angeles in 2019, he asked me about this book. He was curious about how I was progressing with my writing and encouraged me to ask him questions to spark thinking and ideas for the chapters. On this day, I wanted him to tell me about when we left Chicago. So, I asked, "Why in 1974 did we move from Chicago back to Canada? And why to the small town of Belleville?"

His answer surprised me and taught me more about Bob Proctor, the man and father. He said he was tired of always being on the road and wanted a simpler life for himself and his family.

The funny thing is that Dad loved to work – it was his purpose and passion. In fact, it was when he was not working that he would get restless. So, that short-lived move to Belleville ended up not being about a simpler life; instead, it became about taking time to reflect and examine priorities.

I think he was tired. He worked hard, and in my memory, he was always working. The man you saw on stage was very much the man I grew up with.

Dad liked to tell a funny story about my younger brother Raymond. Whenever someone asked Ray what it was like to grow up with Bob Proctor, Ray replied, "Every dinner is a seminar." Which was true. Dad's passion did not turn off at home. He wanted us to understand and apply the material he was learning and teaching as much as he wanted you to.

Once we made the move to Belleville, Dad quickly discovered that small-town living was not for him and it definitely was not the place to build a business base. He wasn't in sync with his inner self. So, eight months later, we moved to Toronto and to a larger market with more opportunities. My father needed to get back on track with his purpose. But this move to Toronto was made with a lot of intention around the needs of everyone in the family.

I admire him for following his dream without sacrificing his family's needs.

The persistence it took to build his business and reputation to where he was when he passed at 87 is extraordinary, and it truly speaks to his strength of character.

In the late 1960's, the concept of self-development was new and not widely understood, very different from today. He worked long hours, and much of the time, we just got by. There were many struggles in those early days, many rejections. People were not open to the idea of self-improvement. It wasn't something the greater population was even thinking about. Trying to sell and teach professional and personal development in those early days was like swimming upstream.

But Dad remained committed to creating value. He knew the information that had changed his life would help others. He knew it was the ticket to meaning and fulfillment.

When I was young, Dad would return home from a long day, and remind me that persistence plays a role in every success. I think that by reminding me, he was reminding himself.

"Persistence is a unique mental strength essential to combat the fierce power of repeated rejections and numerous other obstacles that sit in waiting." Dad could say this with such conviction because he was experiencing it.

In the beginning, before we moved to Chicago, Dad was working in Toronto as a distributor for Nightingale Conant. This meant he was lugging around a heavy case door to door that was filled with records and printed material. I remember him saying one night that he was going to find a way to sell these products – or we would be eating them! That is when it struck him that what he needed to be doing was not focusing on the products but instead selling the idea of how these products could create change.

Despite the obstacles early on, young Bob Proctor always had a vision of what his life and business would grow into. He kept focused on his big, scary, and exciting goal, and he took action every day. After he'd had that realization about selling the idea of change, it wasn't long before he was the top distributor for Nightingale Conant.

When I asked about Chicago that day at breakfast, he told me that it wasn't always easy, but it also wasn't hard – because he loved it. And that every rejection and bad day was worth it – in fact, they were necessary.

He reminded me that when we walked into the seminar room that day in Los Angeles, he would see the fruits of his labor in front of him. First, he had seen it in his mind, and now he was seeing the physical manifestation of that vision and goal.

That belief that everyone needed this information never changed for him. That is what this work has always been about for my father; helping people to understand that they possess greatness and can create real and meaningful change in their life.

CONSIDER...

Can you think of a current or past challenge in your life?

We often only realize what we are capable of when we are challenged. That is when we understand that we are capable of much more than we ever realized.

I have an exercise for you. Write out a challenge you have had in your life or one that you are currently dealing with. Include your thoughts and feelings about it. Include how it made you feel and how you feel about it now.

Next, make a numbered list of 1-5 and add five things you learned from that challenge. Now add the numbers 6-10 and list five things you will do differently because of what you learned.

Leave that on your desk and look at it each day for a week. Can you add to your list? Do you see how the challenge was an opportunity in disguise?

What I Know

Watching my Dad over the years, seeing the struggles, witnessing his commitment and persistence despite losses, plus his wins... ingrained in me that we can become our greatest desire if we hold onto our vision despite outside circumstances and failures.

You're capable of more than you may think. Use all the challenges and changes you experience as tools and learn to look forward to every experience in life as an opportunity to learn and grow.

NOTES:

All About The Chalkboard

*"Form the habit of always
doing your best."*
— Bob Proctor

Long before computers and PowerPoint, my Dad turned to classroom tools to help him deliver his message visually. If you have seen any YouTube videos of the *You Were Born Rich* program, then you know what tool my father used to visually get his message out while speaking… it was a chalkboard.

He was an artist with that chalkboard. When he drew a circle to represent the mind, it had to be flawless. It was art in the making to watch him draw that circle on the board using the side of a piece of chalk. Not only was the teaching invaluable, but watching him use that prop was pure entertainment and, in my mind, genius. I had watched him practice making that circle over and over and over for years until he felt he could do it with one movement and that it flowed exactly with his delivery and timing.

When Dad was teaching, it was essential to him that he be able to convey his message as simply as possible so that anyone could understand and apply it. That was part of his effectiveness and influence; it was his brilliance. That chalkboard was his partner in transferring his message. He would explain to the audience how he saw the mind of everyone sitting in that room as a clean slate like the chalkboard, and if it wasn't a good image, they wouldn't get a good picture.

In the beginning, when he conducted a seminar, he would use whatever chalkboard the venue had on hand. Unfortunately, they were usually small and cheap. And it was tough to get those boards clean because the surface was worn out and typically pretty beat up.

I remember Dad getting frustrated with the quality of those boards, and he decided it was time to invest in his own. In no time, he had a high-quality chalkboard made precisely to his specifications without considering how we would transport this thing from seminar to seminar. The final creation was big; it was 6 feet wide and 4 feet high, cumbersome and heavy! He also had a unique (and heavy) stand constructed that the board would sit on. He then had an enormous crazy-looking metal container welded together that went on a roof rack so that he could transport that chalkboard on the roof of his car.

He reached a point where he would not go anywhere without that chalkboard if he was going on stage. It didn't matter how far away the next venue was. He was on the road with that crazy contraption on top of the car.

Not only was this thing awkward to carry, but if it was windy outside, it could really pull you around a parking lot. Add Toronto snow and biting cold to the equation, and you have the makings of a comedy skit. You risked frostbite if you weren't careful and touched the metal frame around the board without your gloves. We got plenty of looks hauling that thing around and had plenty of laughs.

The other non-negotiable for Dad was the dustless chalk and very specific towels he needed. He ordered the towels from a beauty supply chain, and Gina carried a large case of that chalk in her vehicle at all times. Dad would clean the chalkboard with his special towels at least 8-10 times during a 3-hour event. But, again, the images he drew on that board represented the audience's mind, and that board had to be spotless so he could draw the perfect image. And that is where the towels came in. They needed to be moistened exactly right, not too wet, not too dry, so they would effectively clean the board and allow it to dry quickly, and he could use it immediately after cleaning. And only Bob Proctor knew the perfect water/cotton ratio needed to execute this operation. I'd often see him leaning over the back of the stage, wringing out towels Gina and I had prepared in advance.

In those days, we frequently held preview seminars at the same hotel in the northwest end of Toronto. These were free events that anyone could attend. Dad would teach for roughly 3 hours and then promote an upcoming program that would run one night a week for the following 8 weeks. Oh, how the internet has changed things...

When preparing the room, Gina and I would set up the chalkboard on the stage and position it just as he liked, or so we thought. We would tweak its position and angle until we felt we had it right. Then, we would stand at the back of the room and smile when he came in before the event started. We would watch Dad go on the stage, set out his books, and look around. Without fail, he would adjust that chalkboard by an inch. We came to understand that he needed to make that final adjustment. He needed to be the last to touch it – that chalkboard was his friend and partner; it was his vehicle for transporting his message.

Years later, when the chalkboard was long gone, Gina and I shared with Dad our version of the chalkboard circus and his peculiarities with it. He had a great laugh over that one. I called Gina when I wrote this story, and we had so much fun looking back at that time together. She reminded me that we were witnessing the building of greatness. Everything counted with Bob Proctor. Everything.

This is a fun story to relive and drives home a powerful lesson. Dad was a perfectionist when it came to communicating this work. He was serious about his craft. So, when it came to teaching material that he knew could really impact a person's life, everything had to be prepared and ready to work together like a practiced symphony. You may have thought you were about to hear a motivational speaker when you attended one of Bob Proctor's seminars, but within the first 30 minutes, you knew you were in the presence of one of the most effective teachers alive in the area of the mind and paradigms. Every aspect of his presentation was practiced (not rehearsed) and perfected. And what drew people in and made each presentation he gave a unique experience is that he used his intuition and the audience's energy to direct him on how he taught each lesson; it was never rote. It did not matter if he was having a bad or good day; you got the very best he had that day. And, up until his passing, before getting on stage, he would sit in a comfortable chair, relax, quiet his mind and ask for guidance to have the right words for the audience he was about to present to. My father was the consummate professional.

What strikes me even now is that he gave his best in even the smallest details. But as he would often share, the small things make the big things great!

CONSIDER...

What little thing can you do today that will make you more effective?

Remaining committed to your goals and overcoming inevitable obstacles takes work. When you hit the obstacles, bring your focus to what you can do right here, right now, at this moment. All actions in the right direction count, no matter how seemingly small.

Specifically, in moments of challenge, you want to recognize what you are grateful for. The moment you acknowledge the good, you put yourself into a higher vibration.

As we have all heard Bob Proctor say, "You are likely only one step away from greatness."

NOTES:

Rose Colored Glasses

"No one is in charge of your
happiness except you."
- Bob Proctor

I tend to look at life and the world through rose-colored glasses. Because I view life this way, I am often accused of not being a realist. To my detractors, I say - I live a much happier, healthier, and more productive life because of this conscious choice.

There are always at least two ways to look at something. If you try and see the value in everything, my experience has been that you will attract good into your life because of that choice.

On the other hand, I have been with people who only see the negative in every situation or constantly look for what's wrong and are always ready to tell you about it. Those folks are never pleased and seem to attract precisely what they are focused on – the negative. But, of course, when you are in that vibration, negative is all you will see, so of course, it is what you will attract.

Once in a meeting, Dad said, "Any dummy can tell me what's wrong. I want someone to think and tell me what's right." It made me chuckle, but there sure is truth in that.

Dad often taught an exercise about the power of writing something out 100 times a day. It could be a gratitude statement or a desired outcome that you wish to manifest; it was whatever the mind needed to be trained to see.

He would explain how this is similar to the way you would train your muscles by working out. You don't go to the gym once and expect a well-toned body; it takes discipline and repetition. But, like your body, you can train your mind. And when you train your mind to look for and find the good and use your will to live this way, you will feel lightness in your life and you will find that you are better able to handle the things that may have gotten under your skin before. When you are looking for the good in every situation you can better regulate your emotions. You can choose a different response. It is not about repressing, it is about transforming yourself with a new approach and attitude.

I know I attract more good into my life because I choose to live this way, and you can too. People are attracted to positive energy and want to deal with and be around someone with positive energy because of how they feel when they are with you. It makes you physically and mentally more attractive. Opportunities will flow your way because of your outlook.

Since I was young, I have watched my father respond to situations and rarely react. No matter what it is, good or bad, he would lean into the good. That is where he chose to live, and because of his example, I do too.

Once while discussing an issue that was dominating the news, the first thing Dad said to me was that something good must come out of it. He went on to discuss universal laws and specifically the Law of Polarity.

According to the Law of Polarity, everything is dual. Things that appear to be opposites are actually two inseparable parts of the same thing. Think of hot and cold, for example. Although they're opposites, they're on the same plane, and you cannot have one without the potential for the other. You can think of anything you want to attract in the same way. For example, abundance is inseparable from poverty, love is inseparable from misery, and success is inseparable from failure. Each comes with the potential for its opposite.

The best way to apply this principle is to write down any negative you are currently experiencing and then write down the opposite. Once you have the opposite, it is just as easy to give energy to your desired outcome as it is to the negative. It requires discipline to focus your mind on the desired thought and when your mind wanders to the negative side, you gently bring it back. This is how you create change. This is training your mind.

I'm not saying undesirable things won't happen just because you look at life through rose-colored glasses. However, whatever is not good won't last as long, and you will find a better way of getting through it. It comes down to the age-old expression of looking at a glass half-full or glass half-empty.

You may have heard my father refer to his friend, Reverend Michael Beckwith, who runs the Agape Church in California.

During one of their conversations, Michael said that when something we perceive as bad happens to us, we need to approach it in the following manner:

1. It is what it is; Accept it (It will either control you, or you will control it).
2. Harvest the good (There's good in everything; seek and you will find).
3. Forgive the rest (Forgive means letting go of completely; abandon and release).

Dad loved how Michael phrased this. In fact, he loved it so much that he had Gina create a wooden desk plate beautifully engraved with those words, and we gave them out at seminars.

When you decide you want better in your life, go out into the world and put on your rose-colored glasses. Start with today. Say to yourself, "Today is the day I will look for, find and focus on the good in every situation."

CONSIDER...

Ask yourself what your 'set point' is.
How do you move through your days?
Do you tend to see only the negative,
or do you look for the positive?

If you have chosen to look at life from a more positive perspective, you know the lesson here and what an excellent way it is to live. However, if you are someone who sees the wrong in everything, then I encourage you to start with one day at a time and pause before you attach meaning to each thing in your day. Write a reminder in a place where you will see it throughout the day; a word that triggers your focus. Pay attention to how finding the good makes you feel, how the people around you respond, and – more importantly – how your world begins to shift because of how you see it.

What would your life be like if you
trained your mind to focus only
on your desired outcome?

Your mind is the master architect of your universe. I am sure you have heard the phrase – "Be careful what you wish for." There is truth in this. It is easy to focus on what we don't want or, worse, to spend precious time and energy focusing on the outcomes we are afraid of. Think of the times you have done that – obsessed with the idea this 'could' happen. Did it happen? My guess is no.

The worst we imagine rarely happens, yet we waste our precious time and energy worrying about the worst.

Think about creating your future by design – where you are the architect. Tune into your desires, set your intentions, and, most importantly, take control.

You absolutely can shape your life. Begin today.

NOTES:

It's Possible The Answer Is Right In Front Of You

*"Be open to receiving
the good that you desire."*
— Bob Proctor

Many years ago, I lived in a small beach community just Northwest of Vancouver, British Columbia. I lived on Howe Sound, and for me, it was magical. It was the first time I had ever lived on the West Coast.

This way of living was new to me, and it resonated deeply with my soul. As a child, I was attracted to television shows about nature, and I have always had a passion for fishing and a deep love and connection to the water. Living this way was something I had dreamt about for as long as I can remember. I was embracing this opportunity.

I found a beautiful home to rent for a year to get a feel for the area. The gentleman I rented the house from told me I could catch prawns right out front. He left me a trap, 300 feet of rope, a buoy, and a canoe so I could get started with paddling out and setting the trap.

I made learning everything I could about catching prawns my first goal – how to bait the trap, the depth to place the trap, and so on. Unfortunately, my initial attempts didn't go well. I consistently set the traps too deep, and pulling them up off the bottom was difficult while working to stay balanced in a canoe. Sometimes I would get two or three prawns, and other times the trap would be empty.

A neighbor nearby frequently watched my efforts, and whenever he had the chance, he told me I was wasting my time. He insisted that prawns were no longer in the inlet.

I persisted. A big part of why I continued was that my father trained me to follow my desire and stay focused on my goal. Knowing Dad would tell me to persist, I persisted.

After a week or so, I landed on a few areas that started to produce. Sometimes, I would pull the trap and find 20 or 30 prawns. To me, this was a win. After that, I started marking my locations and created a strategy.

In no time at all, each day, I was pulling up traps filled with prawns. This abundance allowed me to share with others and to also trade with salmon fishermen for their fresh fish. This lifestyle was very satisfying, and knowing I figured it out when others around me thought it wasn't possible made me proud of myself.

A special memory I have from this time is the company of seals that seemed to show up from nowhere and stuck close when I paddled out in the quiet early mornings to check the traps. These curious marine mammals frequently came in close to check what I was doing. There was always one seal in the group that was easy to identify from its unique markings of light skin and a specific pattern of spots on its face. It also had deep, dark, curious eyes; this seal enjoyed making eye contact. I could easily spot this one in the crowd. I named it Pup.

This little seal would follow me and watch me closely as I pulled up the traps and dropped them back down. It really made for an enjoyable time when I was out on the water. I spoke softly to Pup and felt a friendly bond between us. It was a confusing time in my life, and this connection brought me peace.

On one particularly miserable winter day after a storm, I went out when there was a break in the weather to check on the traps. The storms had kept me off the water for several days. The water was very choppy, so being in a canoe was tricky. I had to really focus on not tipping over.

When I got to the first trap and started to pull it up, the wind picked up. It pushed the canoe adrift while I was still pulling. After I got the trap into the canoe and emptied it out, I put in fresh bait and then paddled back to where I thought my spot was to drop it. I had to work fast because the wind was gaining strength, the waves were getting bigger, and a bit of fog was rolling in.

The conditions made it hard to judge the distance to shore. I sent the trap over the side and fed the rope out. When the rope reached its length, it usually would stop, but this time it kept feeding out. It was moving so quickly that it was impossible for me to grab and control it without tipping over. The entire 300 feet of rope went out and pulled the buoy, dragging it under the surface. Under the circumstances, there was nothing I could do. For safety, I had to get myself back to shore.

The storm lasted several days, so all I could do was sit at my window and watch. I thought for sure that I had lost the trap.

After about a week, the skies cleared. So, I rigged up a long pole with a hook on the end of it, figuring that I could paddle out and hopefully see the buoy submerged in the sunlight and reach down to hook it and bring everything back up.

I paddled around for over an hour without any sign of the buoy. I really felt turned around. I looked where I thought I had dropped it, and there was no sign of it. Pup was swimming alongside me the entire time and was the only seal to join me that day. I searched for over two hours and finally gave up.

Pup left my side and swam out to deeper water as I began paddling back to shore. I could hear the seal barking out on the water when I was almost to shore. That was not unusual. But what was unusual was its behavior; the seal was swimming in fast circles.

As I began pulling the canoe onto land, Pup began barking more rapidly and splashing while it swam in circles. I thought to myself, "There is no way!" However, I listened to my intuition and that seal and thought, "I need to be open to possible answers right in front of me."

Jumping back in the canoe, I paddled my way out to where Pup was swimming in circles. It was much further out than I would ever go to drop the traps. However, the storm had played tricks on my sense of orientation. As I came closer to the seal, the water was clear and I could see the buoy! Pup was circling it with an exaggerated motion; the buoy was sitting about six feet below the surface.

I got a hold of the traps with the pole I had rigged up and got everything back into the canoe. I thanked Pup both outwardly and inwardly. It was a moment with nature that I will never forget. That neighbor from a few doors down was out on his deck and witnessed it. He told me he had never seen anything like that in his life. From that day on, the locals called me *the Seal Whisperer*. I kind of liked that.

I often reflect on this experience and lesson with gratitude. I am grateful I persisted and that I allowed the possibility of something unexpected.

During my year in British Columbia, when Dad was doing back-to-back programs in BC, he and Gina came to see where I was living. I remember them both sitting on the deck in the sunshine. I made a nice dinner for the three of us. I was so happy to have them there.

Although I know this way of living is not something my father would ever choose for himself, I appreciated how he supported me. He asked me questions that told me he was not only curious but really had no idea why anyone would want to live so far out of the city. Dad used to say that he could live in a hotel. He loved hotels – the service, the amenities, and the convenience. The way I was living was definitely not convenient. But he supported me despite not understanding it and was happy for me.

CONSIDER...

What does it mean to stay open to possibilities?

Essentially, it is a willingness to keep an open mind and to listen to different ideas, opinions, and thoughts. Consider other possibilities.

Are you open to an answer that may be right in front of you?

When you stay open to possibilities, you see the opportunities. You gain fresh insights and will learn new things about yourself.

Saying yes to new opportunities and ideas will grow your mind and feed your soul.

NOTES:

Dad receiving the Legacy Award from Cynthia Kersey in
2016 at the Unstoppable Foundation Gala
in Los Angeles

Act As If

" What others think of you
is none of your business."
– Bob Proctor

Freedom comes when we stop being what other people think we should be and start acting like the person we want to be.

Have you ever heard the saying that if you tell yourself a lie often enough, you will start to believe it? The basic premise is that your subconscious mind will accept whatever you impress upon it, unlike your conscious mind, which can reject thoughts and ideas. Your subconscious (emotional) mind only accepts the images you feed it with emotion and repetition.

As far back as I remember, Dad would say, "Brian, act as if you are already the person you want to become." He said it because he knew that if I learned to create from within that, the subconscious mind would not know the difference between fact and fiction; and if I acted like the person I wanted to become, I would eventually become that person. This holds true for all of us.

It was Alfred Adler, the Austrian medical doctor, psychotherapist, and founder of the school of individual psychology, who first coined the phrase, '*Act as if*'. It was in the 1920's, and he developed a strategy for his clients to practice roles that differed from their dysfunctional behaviors or realities. It is often called role-playing.

Dad taught me a lot about using behavioral tools to improve my reality. I often hear people mock the catchphrase – Fake it until you make it – which comes from the idea of 'Act as if'. And I get the cynicism because when used literally, the term can conjure up a sense of someone being a total impostor trying to lie or cheat their way to success.

However, these claims are missing the point of this exercise. Acting as if is about changing your behavior to align with the person you are working to become. Changing your behavior, first, will change what you feel and how you think about yourself.

My father and his suits are a good example of this. For as long as I can remember, Dad has had a love for fine-tailored suits.

Back in the early 1960's, when he first started his cleaning business, he scraped together his last few dollars to buy a wool suit. This was the one and only suit he had for his first few years in business. It was not of high quality, so you can imagine how scratchy it would start to feel on his skin. He loved the look of it but got tired of how it felt and more importantly, he got tired of the same look every day.

Well one day, he heard an interview on the radio with someone famous. It came out that this person had over 20 custom-tailored suits in his closet! That really shook my father. He thought to himself, "How wonderful would that be?" Until that time, he had never heard of anyone with more than one, maybe two suits.

Something in that interview changed Dad's perspective.

He decided then and there that if he reached a specific target each month, he would go out and get himself a custom-tailored suit. He honored that agreement he made with himself, and it wasn't long before he had a closet full of suits.

In the beginning, he had to act like the person that deserved and could afford all those suits. But in no time, he became that person. You would be hard-pressed to find him dressed in anything else.

Wearing these well-made suits not only changed how he felt about himself, it changed the way he carried himself. I remember him telling me that wearing those new suits made him walk with purpose. He knew that the people around him started to see him differently too, and he liked that.

Being dressed this way was a very important part of how Dad saw himself, and because he understood how dressing this way positively affected his self-image, he wanted others to have the same experience. So he began giving custom clothing as gifts and rewarding people that worked for him with custom suits or dresses. He continued that tradition right up to the end.

As a result, we were a very well-dressed company and family.

I grew up understanding that you cannot cherry-pick which of the universal laws you will live by. They all apply, and you either live your life consciously following all of them, or you don't. And if you don't, you will never experience growth in a way that serves your entire being.

You may appear to be winning because one area of your life is giving off that appearance, but the truth is if you are not living in alignment with all universal laws, you are not winning.

Acting as if doesn't mean being phony or inauthentic. It's about changing behavior first. It is a step toward changing the way you see yourself. The goal is to change how you feel inside. And you will know you are on track when you feel that change. Feeling is the language of the subconscious.

In January 1988, I started a new career as a real estate salesperson. Dad had two suggestions that I applied immediately:

1. Act as if I am the most successful real estate salesperson ever. If I do, people will believe it, and more importantly, in time, so will I.

2. Only surround yourself with successful salespeople.

That was some of the best advice I ever internalized. I made sure I started in an office with successful people and stuck closely to them, learning from them. I acted like I was selling a house every day and had been doing it forever. My very first clients would have never known that they were my first ever real estate sale. The key was that I gave them service far superior to anything they had experienced before, so in their eyes, I was the successful agent I acted like, and it didn't take long for my self-image to catch up.

When I had close friends or family try and knock me down, I would just let their comments go without giving them energy. As Dad would say, "They don't know any better. Just forgive them and keep going." So, I stayed in character, and soon, I was exactly who I was acting as. In my first year, I made it onto the top 100 list for a major real estate company nationwide.

For me, this was not an experiment. It was a way of life that I had been brought up with, and it has always worked for me.

When you define the higher version of yourself you are reaching for and begin to live this exercise, you will stand taller, smile more broadly, move confidently, and, in every respect, act as if you own it.

Jim Rohn coined the phrase, "You are an average of the five people you spend the most time with." This is so true. Who are you surrounding yourself with?

Dad loved putting that quote up on the screen during his seminars, saying that – if you surround yourself with people who are making it happen – people who are going in the direction you want – just surrounding yourself with them is a step toward your path of improvement. And he'd follow that up with – you need to keep company with people who are positive and supportive of you and who are out in the world making a difference. I absolutely believe this is true.

I often reflect on my father's strength. It wasn't until the end of his life that he admitted his early fears of failing.

In the beginning, putting on seminars took a lot of work and was not always profitable. Leaving behind a successful cleaning business that he had built into an empire serving several cities and countries to pursue his dream of teaching this material really opened him to criticism and self-doubt. He told me that in those moments, he turned his focus and energy to teaching the information that had enabled him to build that empire in the first place.

Teaching from the stage was all he wanted to do, so when he would show up to speak and the audience was small, he taught as if every seat was occupied.

I will never know exactly how long it took for my father to become the full version of what he imagined, but I know it was years. And because Dad was always working to improve himself, he likely changed that image many times… always adding to his definition of what he wanted next for himself, the person he wanted to become. He never stopped reaching for new heights. Even at the age of 87, in the days that preceded his death, he was studying and working on himself.

Whenever I feel doubt creep into my thoughts, I take a quiet moment and think to myself, "What would my father do?" I then commit to having the kind of persistence and discipline he showed me my entire life.

CONSIDER...

Decide that you will be the one to define who you are. Not others.

What we give attention to in our life grows. So be careful and purposeful about what you are focusing on. And always remember that negativity keeps company just as much as positivity does. You get to choose the company you want to keep.

Maintaining the vision.

Keep in mind that to - Act as if - when you are not there yet is not always easy to do because we all have friends and family who have their stories about who we are. To present them with a different version of us is uncomfortable. In fact, often, when we try to be something different, those closest to us will be the first ones to try and bring us down. They do this because they feel threatened. They may or may not even realize what they are doing.

It is like my Dad would say… "People don't resist change; they resist being changed." And when you present yourself differently to those close to you, you are making them uncomfortable; you are shifting their world and creating change.

This is the real test - when you enter this phase of judgment from those you love and are close to. How bad do you want this?

When we feel judged becomes the moment in time when we need to hold tight to our vision and act with confidence and determination to be that better version of ourselves – regardless.

The ability to hold the vision and - Act as if, despite how it feels when the sharpness of others opinions cut deeply – is when you know you are aligning your behavior with your belief.

NOTES:

Choose Wisely

*"While you don't get to choose
your relatives, you can — and should —
choose everyone else."
— Bob Proctor*

Lloyd Conant, Leland Val Van De Wall,
Dad and Earl Nightingale

As mentioned earlier, one of the critical things my Dad taught me was to surround myself with people who would cause me to think better, act better, and be better. He would say, "Brian, you never want to be the smartest guy in the room. Instead, you want to be surrounded by people that will cause you to stretch."

Think about it... attitudes and behaviors are contagious, and the people you surround yourself with will impact your life in a way that can make or break it.

Around the time I was born, my father met a man named Ray Stanford. Ray was likely the first truly successful person who mentored Dad. He was certainly the first to show interest in helping him become a better man.

As their friendship grew and Dad implemented what he was learning from Ray, he noticed that he was attracting other good people into his life. And as this happened, his awareness grew, and his life elevated. For the first time ever, my father began deliberately choosing with whom and how he would spend his time. I remember him telling me how it made him feel to finally understand that he was in control of his life. It gave him hope.

Dad was an action-taker. Let me give you an example of what I mean. For years, Dad listened to recordings of Earl Nightingale every day. With his hand, he would hold a portable record player and listen to *Lead the Field* and *The Magic Word* while driving in his car. Those were some of the first recordings Earl had ever made. He had listened to these recordings so often that he could recite them word for word. Earl was becoming one of Dad's mentors without knowing it. So, after a lot of time spent reprogramming his subconscious mind with Earl's teachings, he decided it was time to meet the man who was so profoundly affecting his life.

It was 1971 when Dad made a bold move that changed direction of his developing career. He cold-called Earl Nightingale's office in Chicago and asked to speak with him. Earl was not there, but the secretary took his number and said she'd have him return the call. Well, much to his surprise, Earl Nightingale did call him back! When Dad answered the phone, he heard Earl's rich, deep voice say what he'd heard him say thousands of times at the start of all his recordings: "Hello, this is Earl Nightingale."

He said that hearing Earl's voice on the other end of the phone line sent shockwaves through his body and that he nearly dropped the phone.

Without hesitation, Dad asked Earl to meet with him and said he would happily fly to Chicago to make it happen.

Earl replied that he was busy but that he would arrange for someone from his office to sit down and meet with him. This was not the answer my father was looking for, so in no uncertain terms, he repeated his request and made it clear that the person he wanted to sit down with was Earl Nightingale. And, being the natural-born salesperson my father was, he provided Earl with options of days and times that he could come to Chicago.

Earl chuckled and agreed, and just like that, Dad was sitting across from Earl Nightingale at his desk in his Chicago office. Before I knew it, the family was moving to Chicago. That is how quickly and confidently Bob Proctor took action.

Earl Nightingale and Lloyd Conant became a part of Dad's circle of influence. I was just a young boy when we made that move to Chicago so he could work with these two giants in the personal development industry. As my father would have been the first to say, they didn't just start a company; they started the entire industry. The experience Dad gained working with Earl and Lloyd was the springboard for eventually going out on his own. Dad spoke of the endless flow of ideas he would have while working at Nightingale Conant and how with his office right next to Earl's, he always knew what book Earl was reading, and he would quickly go out and get himself a copy too.

I specifically have fond childhood memories of Lloyd Conant and being at his house for dinners. He felt like a grandfather to me. It was Lloyd who really taught my father the power of marketing and salesmanship.

Dad had another very close friend whom he spent a lot of time with while in Chicago; his name was Gerry. It was during this time that the idea of teaching to large groups began to form in Dad's mind. In fact, it was in our home on Maplewood Lane in Glenview, Illinois, while working at Nightingale Conant, that he wrote out his goal on a goal card of becoming a speaker and building a business that operated all over the world.

One day while driving to work, Dad had an inspired idea to record himself speaking as if he was teaching to an audience. This idea excited him and terrified him at the same time. He got started right away making a demo recording. I remember him telling me that he had put a lot of time and effort into making that recording, working and reworking the presentation to get it just right.

He asked Gerry if he would be willing to listen to it. This was a big step, but he was proud of what he had recorded.

The day Dad shared his recording with his friend was a turning point. The two of them sat on the couch in the living room as Dad played the recording. Not a word was said, but the look that this friend gave him said it all. He was embarrassed for my father.

I often think of the courage it took in those early days to keep going. It would have been easy for him at that moment of shame and embarrassment to just say, "Well, it was just an idea," and move on. And he did, for about two hours. But then he realized what he was doing.

He was letting someone else steal his dream simply by the embarrassment and shame he felt after sharing it.

What Dad discovered quickly was that this friend did not support or encourage him. In fact, with a simple look, he knocked him down. After that, Dad slowly put distance between them, and they did not spend as much time together.

Changing the people we spend time with can be difficult because our inner circle often includes close friends or family whom we've known our entire lives. And they are not necessarily comfortable with us changing.

I admire that my father was unwilling to allow anyone, even someone close, to deter him from his goal.

This is an excellent example of why we need to choose wisely who will be in our inner circle. We need to have people that not only support our dream but people who will enhance it by encouraging and challenging us. We also need to be that person for others. Outgrowing the people around us is natural when on a path of personal development. You don't need to cut them out of your life altogether; you just don't visit as often, and you don't spend as long.

I always laughed when I would hear Dad say, "I don't want to spend a lot of time with anybody who is not goal oriented because I might catch what they've got!"

CONSIDER...

Are you surrounding yourself
with the right people?

If you want a preview of your future, look around at the people you are hanging out with.

We will become what we think about most of the time, and what we think about is greatly determined by who we spend the most time with.

Choose wisely.

As you grow, that may mean changing friends and colleagues. It's okay; it's part of life. Just trust that hard work and not getting involved with wrong thinking will keep you on track for reaching your goals.

Begin by listing five people you think could help you take your growth to a new level. These can be people you already know or want to know. They can be people you may never know but can still learn from.

Success will come from keeping your sights on your goals and always working to be better.

NOTES:

A Real Pro

"You don't become a real pro by doing certain things – you become a real pro by doing things in a certain way."
— Bob Proctor

I recently watched a recording of my father hosting the first segment of a Masterclass program he created during the pandemic. Whenever I watch Dad teach online, it helps me to see him the way others see him.

In this segment, he was delivering new content. I know he worked hard to prepare for that new program. When Dad and I would talk in the mornings, he often said, "If I could just reach more people with this information." This was when I knew he was working and reworking his delivery, always striving to say things in a way that more people would understand.

Dad built his presentations with this quote by Albert Einstein as his guiding principle:

"If you can't explain it simply, you don't understand it well enough."

I wonder if people realize how much time my father would put into creating every class and seminar. It would be impossible to know unless you spoke to him daily like I did; you wouldn't have otherwise known because my father was such a pro that he made it look easy.

Dad worked on every presentation as if it were his first. He was constantly tweaking and working on his delivery and visual tools, always striving to impact more people. For example, I remember a slide he had created on vibration. He had found a way to layer the slides to show how vibration moves from one level to another. He was so excited about this, and I laugh when I think about how many times he showed me that slide.

You see, the truth is Bob Proctor never winged it. He would work on a presentation right up to the last minute. Always refining. Often, when he'd send me PowerPoints that he was really excited about, I would think... "these look like the ones you sent me yesterday." But for Dad, creating his PowerPoints was a part of his preparation. He was building a roadmap for the client to follow. And every adjustment had the potential to change another life.

Near the end of his life, when things were more challenging for him, I would suggest he use material from a previous broadcast instead of creating an entirely new presentation. He would look at me like I was speaking a language he didn't understand.

Dad would never let other people help him with his presentations and specifically his PowerPoint slides; I guess those slides were a lot like that chalkboard in the early days. I know Gina tried many times to offer suggestions. And after every event or online class, we would receive emails from people offering assistance to brand Dad's slides to make them look more current. But in all honesty, he didn't care about that. He didn't care if there were different colors or inconsistent fonts. Instead, he created by intuition, and he built each slide in a manner that would best illustrate the concept he was teaching.

Cory would sometimes keep a list of misspelled words she spotted during a presentation, and he would simply laugh when we showed him. Thankfully, Gina would find a way to sneak in the corrections.

This is an example of what I meant when I said my Dad was always a pro, regardless. He was always prepared; he always gave his best – even when there was an easier way by receiving help. He needed the creative process. He knew that was how he would present his best self. It did not matter how he felt or what was happening around him; he made sure he was giving his all, and communicating his message was his priority.

My father would share the following story whenever he was teaching to a group of speakers and life coaches so they could gain perspective and feel better about what they were building for themselves.

It was the early 1970's, and Dad was working to make a name on his own. Guiding him was a clear image of himself speaking from and commanding the stage with large audiences that were willing and ready to receive his presentation.

Dad and David Nightingale (Earl's son) had gone all out and rented an expensive theater in Chicago. It was beautiful, with rows of auditorium seating, rich wood, and an elevated stage at the front. It was just as he'd imagined. It had a few thousand seats, and when he did the onsite visit, he knew this was the perfect place to launch his speaking career.

To fill the theater, he needed a good marketing strategy. With the help of a friend, he created a brochure to use as a direct mailing piece. In those days, you could pay for mailing addresses, and he decided to send 20,000 brochures to homes and businesses in the nearby area. His biggest concern was that he would need more room for everyone when they showed up.

He was more than ready on the day of the event. He had practiced his presentation many, many times and felt confident, excited, and nervous at the same time. To help with the crowd flow, he had hired a few people to help direct people to their seats.

Dad and David were behind the curtain when the doors opened to allow the crowd in. As the start was nearing, David would peek through the curtain, and my Dad would anxiously ask, "How many are there? How many?"

When the time arrived for the presentation to begin, Dad walked confidently onto the stage. Six people had shown up. What made it worse was that those six people were scattered throughout that large auditorium.

Now, what he did next was a testament to his dedication to his dream. Dad commanded the stage and taught as if the theater was packed. He gave that audience of six everything he had; he was a pro, regardless.

That is always how I have known him to operate – 100% full out. And that first theater experience was a real test of character that he would draw upon whenever he faced similar situations throughout his life. He would always show up.

There were many times throughout his career when quitting would have been so easy – but he had eliminated it as an option.

CONSIDER...

How do you show up in life?

How you show up for one thing is how you show up for everything.

A lesson I learned from my father is that instead of trying to label everything as good or bad, accept it as it just 'is'. That way, you don't get stuck in the debilitating thinking of – "why". Accept it and keep moving.

An exercise to try...

Each morning, write out one thing you will do differently that day to improve how you show up for yourself and others. Make notes about how you felt and what you noticed around you when you carried out your intention. Progress happens with practice and commitment to that practice.

This exercise will raise your self-awareness and help you better understand yourself and others. It will empower you.

NOTES:

There Is Always A Way

"When you really want something, and you couple that with an understanding of your nature, of your spiritual being, and the law that governs you, nothing will stop you."
— Bob Proctor

It was during my 15th year in the late 1970's that we were in California. Dad decided it would be fun for my siblings and me to be part of the studio audiences of different shows that were popular at the time.

To this day, I don't know how, but he got us into the audiences of a game show called *The Joker's Wild* and a sitcom that was filming its pilot episode. However, the one I remember most was being at *Johnny Carson's Tonight Show*.

He had arranged tickets for us to be in the audience, but when we showed up, they would not let us in because my sister, brother, and I were all under 18 years old. That rejection set my Dad in motion.

Dad immediately got on the phone and began calling people he knew in the entertainment industry. Finally, he reached a friend who told him that the way to get around the rule of no minors in the audience was to sit backstage. This guy made a few phone calls on our behalf, and in no time, we were guided to the show's backstage and set up in tall chairs right on the floor in direct view of the set. These were the best seats in the studio; we could see everything up close and personal.

It felt so special to be sitting backstage. Johnny Carson was not there that night, but there was a special guest host, Flip Wilson. Flip took the time to come over and personally meet us. He was warm and friendly and had the most beautiful smile. I'll never forget what a lovely man he was. We also had the opportunity to meet Ed McMahon. He also took the time to say hello and ask us questions. It was a magical night.

Years later, we were reminiscing and I asked Dad how he got us in to see the show despite their rules. He replied, "If you really want something, there is always a way to make it happen."

By watching my father, I learned the importance of doing the work to maintain good relationships with people you meet and the people you work with. Dad went out of his way to help the people he knew and to be a good connector. He was always helping friends and others he had yet to meet. As a result, he'd built an extensive network of people worldwide who knew they could count on him.

Through the years, I've watched people meeting my father for the first time, and some were so nervous they couldn't speak. Dad would be open with them and put them at ease with something like, "I'm just like you, and you're just like me; we're no different from one another. So you don't need to be nervous around me or anyone else."

I remember him saying, "If you look at someone like they are better than you, then it is likely that you'll look down on someone you feel is less than you." He was adamant that this was not a good way to live. Instead, we should look at everyone as equal.

Yes, some may have more, some less. Never judge another person's journey. Instead, treat everyone as we would treat ourselves. If we can do that, we can be comfortable in any setting.

A few years back, I was in a meeting with my friend Peggy McColl. She was putting on an event with budding internet entrepreneurs. She had asked if I would be a judge on a panel and listen to people's ideas. Our role was to tell them what we thought and give them guidance, feedback, and encouragement.

While sitting with Peggy, brainstorming ideas, she said, "Why don't we write a book together?"

My first thought was – I'm not sure I could write a book. We then started to discuss options to accomplish what we wanted. Peggy's excitement got me excited and gave me courage. I borrowed her belief. We looked at it from the point of view that the traditional way of writing a book does not have to be our way.

This was a good reminder to avoid getting hung up on, and limited by, how I thought a book was produced.

As we continued talking, we came up with the idea of hosting a series of webinars. In these webinars, we would teach the content we wanted in our book. After making the decision, we promptly set dates, sold the webinars, and led the classes. We recorded everything. We then took the money we earned from the webinars and hired a ghostwriter to take the recordings and organize the transcripts into a book.

There is always a way.

We called the book *Darn Easy: Work Half as Hard, Earn Twice as Much While Living the Life of Your Dreams.* It's about how to make life easier and get into a flow. We had found a way to accomplish the book our way. We even had a large publishing house give us an advance on it because they also liked the idea. This was at a time when it was challenging to get advances on books. The entire process was indeed, Darn Easy!

New paths open when we are willing to consider new ideas and opportunities. So, just like Dad not hearing "no" and finding a different way for us to attend that show, Peggy and I found a better way to make our book work for us.

CONSIDER...

Don't give up.

There is always a way to make it happen. Stay open and look for opportunities. If Dad really wanted something, he didn't hear the word "no."

When feeling challenged with a situation, look at it from different-angles. You may have heard my father say that when he was faced with a challenge, he would write the challenge out on a piece of paper and put it in the center of the table. Then, he would rotate his position around the table, looking at the challenge from what he thought would be the perspective of his long-gone mentors. Stay open to other ways of thinking. Tune into infinite intelligence.

Building your network.

When you meet anyone, look for common ground. That common ground can be found easily by taking the focus off yourself and putting it on the person you are talking with. Ask simple questions, and in no time, you will be able to share a story and a smile. You will realize that we are all the same, just on different journeys.

NOTES:

Uncle Joe

*"Face the thing you fear
and fear will leave you."
— Bob Proctor*

Recently, I heard someone say, "If you don't apply what you've learned, it is just entertainment." I love that phrase because it speaks to the fact that nothing happens without action.

Throughout my sixty years, I have witnessed two types of people who attended my Dad's seminars; those who can recite the information backward and forward, yet the results in their lives never change... and those who take the information, internalize it and take action to apply the material. The difference can always be found in the results, and you can often feel it in a person's energy when you are near them.

One of the most significant examples of someone who resisted and then later applied Dad's teachings came from the most unlikely place... Kingston Federal Penitentiary. Before it was closed for good, this penitentiary was one of Canada's oldest and most notorious maximum-security prisons.

Back in the 1960's, when Dad was new to studying the material of Napoleon Hill and Earl Nightingale, he had a deep desire to share it anywhere and everywhere possible. So somehow, he arranged with the Kingston prison to allow for him to visit the prison one Saturday morning a month to teach to the prisoners. He wanted to show the prisoners that they had the potential to alter their way of thinking in positive ways so that when they left prison, they would not return. There was a movement toward reducing recidivism, so Dad's request fit right in.

When I think of Dad talking about facing fears head-on, this is the story that always comes to mind.

Part of the deal my father struck with the prison was that they would allow any inmate who wanted to attend his session into the room, regardless. The administrators felt this was a bad idea, but Dad wouldn't budge on this condition. In true Bob Proctor fashion, he held his position that anyone would be allowed to attend. And they finally agreed.

Dad became known quickly among the inmates partly because he would bring coffee, donuts, and cigarettes into the meeting room for them to enjoy.

Of course, this drew in all kinds of people. Dad truly felt that if he could get them into the room, they would stay because of the information he was sharing. He knew he could potentially change their lives. His hurdle was getting them to listen.

At each monthly meeting, there was the one same guy who would sit at the back of the room on top of the tables. He would swing his legs back and forth in a way that made noise, and he wore an intimidating smirk across his face. He would laugh loudly at my father and make wisecracks about the information he was presenting. His name was Joe.

The warden said that Joe had been in solitary confinement for seven years. They only let him out of his cell for one hour a day to walk the prison yard and get fresh air; and none of the other prisoners could be around him during that hour. The warden referred to him as a "mad dog" and warned my Dad to keep his distance.

Joe consistently created a real disturbance in the room. Everyone was afraid of him, including the guards. He was massive and looked like his life had not been easy. If you saw him on the street, you would definitely cross to the other side.

This man was serving a life sentence for shooting someone during an attempted robbery. The victim he shot nearly died. If the victim had died, Joe would have been put to death, as Canada still practiced capital punishment in those days.

These meetings that Dad held were Joe's opportunity to get out of solitary for an hour or two once a month.

When Dad would tell this story, he talked about how uncomfortable the meetings became with Joe sitting in the back. The disturbances and distractions got so bad that Dad struggled with teaching and keeping the attention of the rest of the group. Joe was the one who was in control of the room. Finally, Dad knew that he had to change what was happening; otherwise, there was no longer a point in making this monthly trip and running these meetings.

Each trip to Kingston Federal Penitentiary was a six-hour roundtrip drive. That alone speaks to Dad's commitment to making an impact. However, that drive also gave him a lot of time to think about the meeting, and his dread would build with each passing kilometer.

He knew he needed to face this issue with Joe, and going through the guards would compromise his credibility with the other prisoners, so he had to find another way. Finally, after three months of being harassed, Dad decided that he had to face this guy head-on in front of the group.

To say that Dad was facing his fear would be an understatement… he feared for his life. Listening to him tell this story, I have often put myself in his position and can only imagine what it must have felt like. You need to know that in the 1960's, my father was a tall, skinny redhead weighing maybe 140 pounds.

When the morning he'd made the decision to deal with Joe came, he started the meeting like he always had. However, Dad stopped talking when the heckling began from the back of the room. The moment of reckoning had arrived. The room went completely quiet as Dad walked past the other inmates and straight to the back of the room. He stopped directly in front of Joe, inches from his big intimidating face.

In the toughest voice he could muster, he looked at Joe and said, "You must be the dumbest bastard I have ever met. If you would take the time to listen to what I'm teaching, you just might learn something."

Joe's face turned a deep shade of red. Dad was so scared that he could feel himself sweating under his wool suit. He had no idea what would happen next, and the guards were not moving.

Pushing past his fear, he went on to say, "I can earn more money in an hour than you could steal in a month, and when I am done here today, I will freely walk out of this prison, get into my nice air-conditioned car, and drive home." Then, looking right into Joe's eyes, he continued: "When I am gone, you will be taken back to your little cell and locked back up."

Joe sat there vibrating with anger; he returned Dad's stare, and the tension was palpable. And then, suddenly, Joe began to laugh hysterically. He must have thought that my father was about as crazy as anyone he had ever met.

Thinking this was it, Dad turned around and started back toward the front of the room, shouting as he walked: "If you take the time to listen, you might just get out of this place and build a nice life for yourself."

Dad walked out of the prison that day with a feeling of relief and pride. He was still in one piece and had faced a fear that most of us will never encounter.

He had no idea what would happen next, but he had dealt with the issue the best he could.

The following month, to his surprise, Joe was no longer sitting on a table at the back of the room. Instead, he was sitting in the front row in a chair. From that day on, if anyone in the room made a sound or negative comment when Dad spoke, Joe would turn and give a stare that quieted the group.

He became Dad's greatest defender, and everyone in the room stayed in line because of him.

But that's not the end of the story. Joe ended up becoming a good friend. He was eventually released from prison, something no one expected. And when he was released, he came to work with my father. Joe even traveled with us to England to help Dad open a cleaning business. He was such a good friend that I knew him as Uncle Joe. And as a child, I had no idea that Uncle Joe had been in prison.

I can still picture Uncle Joe and hear his deep laugh. He was a big, powerful man, and it was easy to see that his appearance often struck fear in people. However, he was nothing but kind in my eyes.

The first time I heard my father tell this story from the stage, I knew immediately who he was talking about. This story is my real-life example of what it means to face fear and once again showed me how committed my father was to teach.

Uncle Joe proved that anything is possible when you want to change. Joe went on to live a productive and happy life. When I think about those early days, I can only imagine how many other lives have been positively altered over the last 60+ years because my father was willing to do whatever it took to share his passion and make a difference.

CONSIDER...

What are you willing to do to push past a fear that is holding you back?

If fear keeps you from moving forward, that fear will grow until you deal with it. It may even get to the point that it dominates your thinking and keeps you awake at night.

When you face the fear, no longer allowing it to control you, it will leave you, and you will automatically feel more confident. That is mental freedom.

Change is going to happen whether we're ready or not - learn to lean into the discomfort.

When faced with fear and discomfort, retreating is the easiest thing to do, but the easiest thing is often not the best thing. Nothing stays the same, and to grow, we must lean into discomfort. Otherwise, fear will sabotage success in all areas of our life.

You are far more powerful and resilient than you think. Just look at the things you have already overcome in your life. Write some of those out here.

NOTES:

CHAPTER 9

REACT vs. RESPOND

It's Just A Piece Of Tin

"Between stimulus and response there is a space. In that space is our power to choose our response. In our response lies our growth and our freedom."
— Viktor Frankl

Little did I know that a lesson I learned from Dad when I was seventeen would be the same lesson I would pass on to my son twenty-nine years later.

Dad had a saying that became my reality one day. He would say, "Either you own the car, or the car owns you."

He was referring to people who buy an expensive car and won't let anyone drive it – including those closest to them. Unfortunately, their misplaced affection confuses their priorities, and they will often pamper the vehicle more than they indulge the important people in their lives — and sometimes even themselves.

My father's Cadillac Eldorado convertible — the car we drove across the country in when I was fifteen — was a beautiful car that Dad thoroughly enjoyed and took a lot of pride in.

I learned to drive in that vehicle. Later, I got my driver's license in it. As far as cars go, it was my first love.

There were many years that my father was on the road more than he was home. When I was a teenager with a driver's license, this was a big perk because — yes, you guessed it — he willingly allowed me to enjoy that extraordinary vehicle while he was away.

During one of his trips, I got into an accident in his car. I drove right into the back of another vehicle. The accident was entirely my fault.

That day I had an exam scheduled at school, and I was running late. So, I jumped into Dad's car, completely distracted by the exam, and sped off. I was driving too fast and doing everything I could to get through the lights, even if they were yellow.

There was a shopping plaza that I had to go around to reach the school parking lot. I wasn't paying attention. Instead, I was scanning the parking lot to the left, looking for a parking spot, and when I looked back, the stop light was a solid red. The car right in front of me had already stopped. It was too late when I saw it, and I had to pump the brakes hard to try and stop. I slid and ran right into the back of the stopped vehicle.

The dread I felt upon impact was like nothing I'd ever felt.

As I got out of the car to check on the other driver, I saw immediately that she was a woman close to my mother's age. She slowly got out of her car. Once she emerged, I saw right away that she did not look angry. Instead, she looked frightened.

She walked straight over to me and hugged me. You can imagine my surprise at her reaction, especially since I was so clearly in the wrong. She was crying and asked me if I was okay. Then she told me that she was okay too. I remember being so relieved and embarrassed. I felt so much shame for the mistake I had just made and the trouble I had caused this woman.

When I looked at the damage I'd caused to her car plus the damage to the front of Dad's car, I felt sick, and then I felt fear. I knew I had to call my father and tell him what had happened. I had no idea how he would react, but my imagination took my worry and fear to new heights. I made myself physically ill thinking about how this might go.

It took a while, but I found the courage to call Dad later that evening. I told him the entire story, and he listened patiently. I explained how it was my fault. I described the damage that his beautiful Eldorado had suffered.

I will never forget his concern and the peacefulness in his voice when he finally spoke. He said, "Brian, you are okay, and the other driver is okay. That's all that matters. The car is just a piece of tin. It can be fixed." Then he said, "It's called an accident because that's what it is. You didn't intentionally go out to wreck the car, so don't let it bother you another moment."

I remember crying after we hung up the phone. I was crying from both the tremendous relief I felt and from the love and tenderness that Dad showed me.

Dad had the car repaired, and life went on. The next time he went out of town, he let me use the car again without hesitation. He didn't dish out any safety warnings. He knew I was a safe driver and had made a mistake. He knew that I was hard enough on myself about this accident, and he didn't want to add any more grief. In fact, he wanted me to free myself from the burden.

My father loved that car, but he didn't let it control him.

We talked about this incident during his last weeks while he was in the hospital. I told him how his love and kindness had impacted me and how it reminded me of what a remarkable man he was. We then laughed about what happened twenty-nine years later after that accident.

I was in Palm Beach, Florida, speaking to a large group of people that I was working with. From the stage that day, I shared my story about wrecking Dad's car and how he responded. I wanted everyone to understand what a great man my father was, but more, to know how congruent he was with the material he taught. He lived it.

Reliving that experience from the stage was fun, and I enjoyed the story as much as everyone in the group.

Ironically, that night I got a phone call from my son saying he had gotten into an accident and wrecked my truck. It was a single-car accident. He was driving too fast in the rain and slid off the road into a telephone pole.

I could hear the worry in his voice. I responded, word for word, exactly as my father had responded to me twenty-nine years earlier. I could feel that my voice was calm and peaceful. Thankfully, Danny hadn't been hurt, and that was the only thing that mattered, not – "the piece of tin."

Many years ago, Dad was coaching a client in a private session and was teaching the concept of Respond VS React. He got an inspired idea to create a coin that a person could keep in their pocket; something that would ignite cells of recognition in their mind by simply touching it.

Gina had the coins manufactured, and we gave them out at events. I have one sitting on my desk right now. Frequently I have conversations with clients telling me they still carry that coin, and they share stories of how it has helped them.

React

The **REACT** side of the coin has raised lettering that you can feel when you touch it to remind you of the rough side of life - how reacting means you are not in control of yourself.

vs. Respond

The **RESPOND** side of the coin is smooth and reminds you that to live a smooth life, you have to choose to respond. By touching the coin, you can create the moment needed to be in control. You don't even need to look at it.

The awareness created around responding versus reacting means you notice when you feel the urge to withdraw, take flight, or lash out, beginning to rise inside you – and you can choose instead to pause. You learn to let it pass through you.

That pause gives you the space to collect yourself, take a breath, and decide how you will proceed.

With practice, this gets easier, and you find that responding instead of reacting will become your natural way of being.

CONSIDER...

Do you react or respond?
Are you in control of your behavior?

When you react, you don't think. A healthy practice to adopt is to pause and ask yourself, "Is what I am about to say or do important, kind, and necessary?" So many things in life resolve themselves by silently counting to ten before responding.

Bob Proctor mastered the ability to stop, check his attitude, and make a choice that aligned with the image he held of himself.

Patience is not inaction.

NOTES:

CHAPTER 10

SELF-CARE

Breathe

*" Calmness of mind
is one of the beautiful jewels of wisdom."
– James Allen*

Dad liked to leave out books for me to discover. There would often be a new one next to my bed on my nightstand. One of those books was *As A Man Thinketh by James Allen*. It was published in 1903 and described by Allen as, "Dealing with the power of thought, particularly with the use and application of thought to happy and beautiful issues. A book that will help you to help yourself."

In essence, this small book suggests that we become what we think about most often. It lays out the effect our thoughts have on the architecture of our life.

Dad was first given this book in 1972, and from then on, he always kept it near him. He was especially drawn to the final chapter, *Serenity*.

While on stage, he would quote from that final chapter, "Calmness of mind is one of the beautiful jewels of wisdom." Indeed, calmness of mind is something we should all strive for.

Over the years, Dad gave countless people an exercise based on the *Serenity* chapter. The exercise was meant to assist in forming a paradigm of calmness and self-control. It was to create an understanding of the power of directed thought.

In 1990, I attended an eleven-day experiential seminar. The week was very physical and included exercises designed to challenge your beliefs and get you out of your comfort zone.

One of the exercises found me climbing to the top of a telephone pole. It was one of those exercises meant to get you out of your own way; to get you out of your head and into the moment.

I was wearing a harness with a safety rope, so I reasoned I wouldn't get hurt. However, my mind was all over the place.

The pole I was climbing was shaky and unstable. But because I've always been a bit of a daredevil, a part of me was excited about the challenge. What made this a little different was that the pole was on the edge of a hill overlooking a valley. It made it seem and feel as if I was much higher than I was. Because of the sway in the pole, the higher I got, the more focused I needed to become. As I got higher, I could feel my fear growing. I quickly realized that I did not have control of my thoughts.

Once I was near the top, I could see the square platform mounted on a swivel that freely moved above me. It must have been at least two feet higher than the last step. This height difference made it tough to get from the last step to standing fully on the platform, which was the goal.

I held the platform with one hand and struggled to gain leverage; it was dicey because it moved and swiveled as I tried to get my foot up and gain stability. Finally, after intense effort and anxiety, I got there, and when I stood up, my entire body swayed and spun, and my arms flailed as I worked to find balance. This made the pole swerve more. I had no control whatsoever.

I knew I was about to fall off... Then something happened that changed the moment. One of the people watching from the ground yelled loudly:

"Breathe!"

I hadn't even realized that I was not breathing; my head was in a frantic state of mind. However, as soon as I heard that command and took a deep breath, my mind focused on my breathing.

When I did this, I stopped swaying and spinning; I found balance. In that instant, my head became clear and calm. I gained control of my thoughts which gave me control of my environment and my body, and I was able to complete the challenge as long as I kept bringing my focus back to my breath.

It is easy for me to tap into the memory of that experience. And it usually comes up when I am dealing with a challenge and my mind is all over the place. The first thing I notice is that I am holding my breath. When I find myself there, I close my eyes and put all my attention on my breath. I stay there until I feel a sense of calm wash through me, and I feel like I have regained control of my thoughts.

The exercise I mentioned at the beginning that my father gave to clients, friends, and family was to commit to 30 days of taking paper to pen and writing out the *Serenity* chapter from *As A Man Thinketh by James Allen*. He would also suggest that you recite it aloud while looking in the mirror after writing it. If someone said they did not have time, he would say, "Set your alarm to wake 15 minutes earlier each day and, most importantly, commit." Dad did not believe in excuses. This exercise is a no-cost, no-risk way to develop your understanding of discipline, thought, self-control, and calmness of mind.

The changes this exercise can produce are profound. I have seen it myself.

One example that comes to mind is a client I met for the first time in Los Angeles. This man was an accomplished athlete in a sport that would be similar to what is involved in being a stuntman – very physical. He was all over the place when he attended his first live seminar with us. You could see that his mind was not at ease. He was making others around him uncomfortable. And he could hardly sit in his chair for longer than 10 minutes, and how he moved, spoke, and acted indicated that he was living with a very chaotic mind.

He had such little self-control that he jumped up on stage at one point. Of course, this maneuver made all of us nervous – except Dad. After the seminar ended that day, my father sat at a table with this client – just the two of them. Dad gently talked to him about a journey of self-control. He gave him the James Allen book he'd been carrying in his briefcase, asked him to begin writing out the *Serenity* chapter every day for 90 days instead of 30, and asked him to start the next day. He gave him his cell phone number and asked this client to text him at the end of each week. This was to keep him accountable.

Several months later, I ran into this client at another seminar. Although his energy was still high, he had more self-control; he was much easier to talk with. His smile was warm, and he appeared more at ease.

He took out the journal to show me he had done the work. His notebook was filled with chapters of *Serenity* written in entirety, in his handwriting, and he was getting ready to keep going with a fresh notebook.

This client was a great example of the power of a simple exercise to gain control of – and calm – your mind. This was the first step that provided him direction and set him on a path to understanding that he had the power to help himself within himself, changing his way of thinking forever.

At different points in my life, I have committed to this exercise myself, and in writing this, I realize I want to do it again. Calmness of mind is a feeling like no other. You feel powerful because you are in control of your thoughts and responses instead of reacting and feeling bounced around by outside circumstances. This exercise and, ultimately, living with a calm mind creates order out of chaos and clears the way for us to become what we think about with greater intention.

I am going to include that chapter here for you. Keep the publish date in mind as you read this, and don't let the gender-specific language bias the strength and intent of the words for you.

Serenity – from *As A Man Thinketh*

Calmness of mind is one of the beautiful jewels of wisdom. It is the result of long and patient effort in self-control. Its presence is an indication of ripened experience, and of a more than ordinary knowledge of the laws and operations of thought.

A man becomes calm in the measure that he understands himself as a thought-evolved being, for such knowledge necessitates the understanding of others as the result of thought, and as he develops a right understanding and sees more and more clearly the internal relations of things by the action of cause and effect, he ceases to fuss and fume and worry and grieve, and remains poised, steadfast, serene.

The calm man, having learned how to govern himself, knows how to adapt himself to others; and they, in turn, reverence his spiritual strength, and feel that they can learn of him and rely upon him. The more tranquil a man becomes, the greater is his success, his influence, his power for good. Even the ordinary trader will find his business prosperity increase as he develops a greater self-control and equanimity, for people will always prefer to deal with a man whose demeanor is strongly equable.

The strong, calm man is always loved and revered. He is like a shade-giving tree in a thirsty land, or a sheltering rock in a storm. Who does not love a tranquil heart, a sweet-tempered, balanced life? It does not matter whether it rains or shines, or what changes come to those possessing these blessings, for they are always sweet, serene, and calm.

That exquisite poise of character which we call serenity is the last lesson of culture; it is the flowering of life, the fruitage of the soul. It is precious as wisdom, more to be desired than gold – yea, than even fine gold. How insignificant mere money-seeking looks in comparison with a serene life – a life that dwells in the ocean of truth, beneath the waves, beyond the reach of tempests, in the eternal calm!

How many people we know who sour their lives, who ruin all that is sweet and beautiful by explosive tempers, who destroy their poise of character, and make bad blood! It is a question whether the great majority of people do not ruin their lives and mar their happiness by lack of self-control. How few people we meet in life who are well-balanced, who have that exquisite poise which is characteristic of the finished character!

Yes, humanity surges with uncontrolled passion, is tumultuous with ungoverned grief, is blown away by anxiety and doubt. Only the wise man, only he whose thoughts are controlled and purified, makes the winds and the storms of the soul obey him.

Tempest-tossed souls, wherever ye may be, under whatsoever conditions ye may live, know this – in the ocean of life the isles of blessedness are smiling, and the sunny shore of your ideal awaits your coming. Keep your hand firmly upon the helm of thought. In the barque of your soul reclines the commanding master; he does but sleep; wake him. Self-control is strength; right thought is mastery; calmness is power. Say unto your heart, "Peace be still!"

226

CONSIDER...

Will you commit to the writing exercise shared in this chapter?

A calm mind creates a mental state of peace, free from agitation, and helps you focus. Calmness can also impact your creativity and allows you to see what is happening around you from a peaceful vantage point; it gives you control over your thoughts and actions and creates space for the good you desire.

On the other hand, when you are not calm, you may find that your energy is frenetic, which repels and makes everything you are trying to accomplish more difficult and chaotic. It is also impossible to attract good into your life when you are living this way.

Don't forget to breathe.

Breathing is the bridge between the conscious and unconscious mind. Whenever your mind becomes scattered, use your breath to connect your mind and body and regain control of your thoughts.

NOTES:

Healthy Mind - Healthy Body

"When you put an idea in the subconscious mind through repetition, it has to express itself through the body. The body is an instrument of the mind."
— Bob Proctor

Our body is our vessel here on earth. And because our body is an instrument of our mind and everything we are experiencing is happening according to our level of awareness, we should work to not only raise our level of awareness but to also do everything we can to keep our body healthy and strong, so we can easily carry out what our mind has imagined. This is how we live our best life. This is how we take part in and enjoy our journey and all it has to offer.

And let's be honest; our thoughts improve when we feel strong, healthy, and good about ourselves. You cannot untie the connectedness of self-image and success. When we feel good, we think good – and when we think good, we act good; this builds confidence, and people are attracted to us because of the positive energy we are putting out.

During our Paradigm Shift events in Los Angeles, Dad would present in detail how our paradigms control everything in our lives, including our weight. Then, he would instruct us in a writing exercise for a healthy mind/healthy body section. One of the statements that resonated with me during this lesson was when he said, "You don't want to lose weight; you want to release it. " His point was that we naturally look for something when we lose it. However, when we release something, we let go of it completely.

To do this exercise:

1. *In the present tense, write a description of your ideal self-image on a card – the weight you want to be; how you'll look and feel. What does healthy, strong, and fit feel like to you? What kind of clothes are you wearing? What kind of activities are you enjoying?*

2. *Use language that is positive and supports you and your long-term success. Commit to this internal dialogue and kick-out negative self-talk when it enters.*

3. *Read your card several times a day and see yourself as already having accomplished what you've written down.*

4. *Get emotionally involved with these ideas. See yourself smiling and enjoying life. Amplify your mental image with emotion.*

5. *Do these things, and you will be building a new model in your mind that replaces the old one. When we marry ourselves fully to a new image in our mind, our body must express it. We will start choosing actions that support this new image on autopilot.*

The transformation happens by law.

At different times throughout my life, I have completed this exercise precisely as I've laid it out here. At the same time as doing this exercise I also honor where I am currently. I do this by expressing gratitude for my current self-image, and I give thanks for all I can do because of my body.

Like most people, however, there have been times when I have not given this part of my life the attention I should have, and slowly, other areas of my life began to slip too.

When I need a reboot, I always go back to the basics. I prefer to keep things in my life simple. Dad taught that overcomplicating things is often a diversion to avoid focusing on the changes we need to make. It also gives us a way to avoid taking responsibility for our results.

So, when I am not feeling good about an area in my life, I start with my body. I have learned over the years that when I feel good in and about my body, the other areas of my life come into order.

For example, I am more likely to have more energy and be productive when I feel better about myself. And this supports my healthy self-image.

When my father was in his 70's, he hired a personal trainer. Even at that age, he knew the importance of having a healthy body. His goal was to ensure his stamina remained high so he could continue delivering this material from the stage and to his last breath.

One of the many things I loved about my Dad was his passion. And he got passionate about this personal trainer and the work he was doing with him. He got so passionate that it wasn't long before he had the entire family working with his coach.

I needed to drive a fair distance four days a week to participate in these workout sessions. And the workouts were intense. However, after some time, I began noticing that the training focused on building muscle and bulking up was different from my goal. As good as I was feeling, this was not fitting into the image of what I wanted. So, I stepped back from his workout routine and started doing more of what aligned with my goals and vision.

Dad enjoyed that the trainer's approach was precisely what he taught regarding any paradigm shift you want to make. The trainer raised awareness through information, action, and repetition and ultimately – results.

Quality and quantity of life are a part of every goal I create, and being active in ways that keep me healthy while having fun at the same time feeds my soul in a way that makes everything I am doing easier.

Even when we are not in the mood, Cory and I will get out of the house and go for a brisk walk or hike. She always says to me, "It's never the wrong choice." I've asked Cory to share a story with you about a lesson Dad taught her about taking care of her body in a way that elevated her thoughts.

From Cory Kelly Proctor:

When I began working with Bob in 2012, I landed in social media. My aim was to build Bob's voice and message across all social platforms. This was a steep learning curve for me, but I loved how much joy it brought Bob. When I began, his Facebook account was at 40k followers, his Twitter was 16k, and he still needed Instagram, LinkedIn and YouTube accounts. Between 2012 and 2016, I managed to take his Facebook following to over one million followers with similar increases across all the platforms I was managing. This really got Bob excited.

Daily, I would call Bob, or he would call me to discuss content for his platforms. He would have me read him the comments so he could give me answers to reply with. We talked every day about the increase in followers - he loved the numbers. Working with Bob this way really showed me his heart and who he was. It brought me so much satisfaction. However, some days he would call me, and I would be stuck. Often it was a wall I had hit with marketing our ads. It didn't really matter what it was; Bob always gave me the same advice. He would say, "Cory, close your computer, go outside, and take a walk. Exercise your body and clear your mind. Don't wear headsets, don't talk on the phone, or even take your phone. Instead, listen to the sounds, smell the smells, and take in the sights. This will shift your energy and open you to thoughts and ideas you cannot get staring at your computer."

I cannot express enough how correct he was. I still follow this advice with any challenge I am having. Going outside and shaking up my energy is never the wrong choice - it is a win/win for my body and mind.

My father knew how important my health and fitness were to my self-image. He saw how connected my performance in life was to how I felt physically, and when I had times of struggle he would remind me to take care of my body.

When I was growing up, I saw myself as an athlete. I loved the challenge of being physical. A story Dad loved to remind me of is the time he beat me in a foot race. And I loved it too because he would laugh his infectious laugh whenever he told it.

We were on vacation in Florida, and Dad and I were out for a morning walk. I would have been about 14 years old. I don't know what got into me, but I challenged Dad to a race. I was a little full of myself and thought I could whoop him.

We made it simple. The race would start from a line on the sidewalk and go the distance of two utility poles. I had on running shoes and shorts, but dad had on a pair of loafers and casual pants… "This is going to be so easy!" I thought.

As we started, I was out in front, and he was playfully taunting me. Suddenly he was laughing, and out of nowhere, he bolted ahead; he ran past me with such speed that I honestly couldn't believe it.

He beat me without question, and we have laughed about it ever since. It is such a fond memory for the both of us that we joked about it for the rest of his life.

Visiting my childhood home on Maplewood Lane in Glenview, Illinois

CONSIDER...

Will you commit to the exercise
in this chapter?

Movement, health, strength, and fitness are different for everyone. The key is finding what is right for you.

As I mentioned at the beginning of this chapter, your body is your vessel for this life. You are the only one who gets to experience it. Make sure the thoughts and images you consciously choose and impress upon your subconscious mind align with what you want for yourself.

Then manage your activities and day to prioritize yourself and this critical part of your life.

Healthy development includes nurturing all that we are - mind, body, and soul.

Make your chosen routine a non-negotiable
by deciding that you will do it daily.

When you tell yourself that you will do something 3-4 days a week or anything like that, you add a decision-making process that cuts into your chances for success. So instead, make one decision: <u>Every day</u>, I will _____ (you fill in the blank.)

NOTES:

Finding My Own Way Of Inspiring

*"Follow your feelings and
get your intellect out of the way."*
- Bob Proctor

Dad wanted me to return to his business with him. But, for a long time, I just wasn't ready. Then one day, after finding success in my real estate career and knowing I had made it on my own in an unrelated business, I was finally ready. It was 1999, and I needed a change.

When I did return to work with my father, I began in sales, and, to be honest, I did not enjoy it. I knew I had to find a better way to contribute while remaining true to myself.

When I was a child, I took notice of the inspiring books and magazines Dad would read. He often left that material out for my sister, brother, and me to discover. I naturally gravitated to this material. I remember specifically enjoying a little pocket magazine called *Bits and Pieces*. It was filled with inspiring quotes and short stories and always left me feeling better for reading it. It also triggered thinking in me.

Later in the year 2000, I found myself visiting one of Dad's business partners in Arizona. One evening we sat discussing what I could do for Dad's company outside of sales that would have an impact and resonate with me. I can clearly remember where I was sitting in his home when I started talking to him about that little magazine that had left a mark on me as a young child. He said to me, "Brian, look at the excitement you are feeling just talking about this; you are on to something."

It was that evening, when brainstorming, that I came up with the idea to start a service that would serve our clients and build our email list.

I imagined that sending our clients a daily inspirational quote in an email Monday-Thursday and concluding with an uplifting story on Fridays could be an excellent way to keep in touch and build an audience. It would also be a way to showcase the many, many people I had met throughout the years who truly had good stories to share. This was long before 'quote of the day' services were all over the internet.

Creating this was the start of something that forever changed our company. However, when starting this, I had absolutely no idea how significant the impact would be and what a difference it would make for my Dad.

If I had known upfront all that would be required to build this service, I might not have done it. Sometimes being naïve about what is required is not bad and doesn't really matter when you are committed to the outcome – to the goal.

When I started on this path, I didn't own a computer; I'd never had one. I didn't even have an email address. Yet, I was beginning something that required both. After setting myself up, I had to find a program to send out emails. This was before all the specialized, web-based programs that are available today.

In the beginning, I sent all the messages directly from my computer. Then, finally, I found a program that would send them one by one but very quickly. It worked; however, they came directly from my personal computer and used my personal internet service provider.

It wasn't long before I was spending all day and night on my computer. The entire process was very manual. Whenever someone wanted to be added to receive the daily emails, they had to email me, and I had to go in and enter each name into the list one by one. Then, I needed to manually remove their name if they wanted off the list.

Right off the bat, I had a few problems that needed solving quickly. First and foremost, this way of emailing was not scalable. As it grew, it required more of my time, and eventually, I worked 16-hour days just doing data entry.

The second issue arose when my service provider cut me off, thinking I was spamming because I was sending out so many emails each day. I needed to prove that this was a legitimate business and the emails I was sending were to people who wanted them. I knew I was onto something good and that this service was providing value. So, through trial and error, I continued to find ways to make it work and keep it scalable while taking advantage of the quickly advancing technology. However, each day it felt like putting out fires. I was barely keeping up.

What I was building also brought me into the affiliate marketing world before anyone even knew what that was. Initially, I began by offering one of Dad's programs to the email subscribers several times a month. I then found other products from outside companies that were in line with our message that I could promote and earn a commission from that promotion.

That reciprocation built relationships where outside companies would also promote our programs, and we would pay them based on their number of sales. This is what affiliate marketing really is – a promotion to earn a commission and build relationships.

The response from all of this helped me understand the power and effect of an email list. But, more importantly, I had created a way for our company to stay in touch with a growing database of people interested in what we were doing.

Today, email marketing is commonplace. But for me, what I was doing was unchartered territory, and it was exciting.

Because I was willing to act on my idea, our company was prepared for an influx of customers when most other companies were not. We were ahead of the curve in our industry, and it made a tremendous difference in how we were able to communicate with our audience.

Dad loved seeing this new and fast way to reach people in real-time. It was inspiring for both of us. Together we could literally measure the difference this was making. We were reaching people in a new and exciting way... People hungry for what Dad was teaching.

It was my willingness to step out and act immediately after that meeting in Arizona, and my commitment to figure it out along the way, that allowed me to create something of immeasurable and lasting value.

Initially, what I was building did not earn large sums of money. However, it did provide a massive amount of psychic income. And what it morphed into became the marketing cornerstone of what our company became. It all happened one step at a time – often with one step forward and two steps back. It took persistence, but I was in love with the idea of serving our audience this way and so was my father.

It wasn't long before I started getting emails from people telling me how a specific quote changed the direction of their day. Others told me how a story took them out of despair and gave them hope again. And others would share how they used my messages in other countries to teach students how to read English while providing them with a valuable lesson. All those emails I received confirmed that what I was doing added value and helped others. This felt good and kept me focused on continuously improving the value of our content.

It was thrilling to have contact with so many people all at once, asking questions and sharing their experiences. Dad often compared it to his very early days of hauling heavy personal development programs door to door and marveled at how much the world had changed.

CONSIDER...

What does it mean to be an action-taker?

If you have an idea, take action quickly. Even if imperfect, you will learn along the way. That is what happened to me.

I am taking action right now. And the process has unfolded and become clearer with each day. I know this action will make a difference not only for my future but for yours as well.

What one thing will you do today to bring you closer to the change you want to make or the goal you want to reach?

Every action counts. "Big" or "small".

NOTES:

Laughing

"Love and respect yourself.
And as you love yourself, you'll
automatically love others."
— Bob Proctor

If you were close to Bob Proctor, you knew he had a great sense of humor and healthy self-love. Because of his self-love, he had an enormous capacity for great love; to love others completely.

Dad was indeed one of the most passionate people you could ever meet. He had a fearless curiosity that drew you to him. It kept him young because he never stopped learning or asking questions. Accompanying that passion was his laugh – it was a laugh that made heads turn and put smiles on faces. Dad knew how to enjoy and how to show that joy. You wanted his light shining on you, and it was never brighter than when he was smiling and laughing.

On stage, Dad would talk about how we had to love ourselves first before we could really love anyone else in a meaningful way.

The audience would laugh when he said, "You should wake up every morning and kiss yourself," and then he'd flamboyantly kiss his hand. He would then have the audience do it. It was a fun exercise, but he was making a point through this gesture that we must love ourselves first. Self-love is the foundation on which all our relationships grow and blossom, and it's the key to personal success. It was easy to notice the people in the audience hesitating at the idea of kissing their own hand in this way, and you could hear how uncomfortable they were in their laughter.

Dad would say, "It's easy to see when a person lacks self-love; just watch how they carry themselves."

Dad's self-love journey evolved with his growing knowledge of himself as a spiritual being. As his self-awareness grew, his perspective on who he was and what he was capable of changed in profound ways.

He studied human potential daily, paid attention to himself, and started to become clear about the potential within him. He would say that he realized one day that he had a lot to offer the world and that he was just as loveable, valuable, and competent as everyone else. That was when he began to see his place in the world differently.

Dad knew that self-image is the base from which all things grow, both personally and professionally, and that self-awareness and emotional intelligence feed into improving one's self-image. I had so much respect for how my father was always working on his own self-image just as much as he coached others to work on theirs.

Watching him and having conversations with him about how he

was discovering new ways to improve inspired me. He helped me to constantly stay focused on loving myself first and to always be reaching toward growth.

I know without a doubt that without a healthy self-love that our self-image will suffer, and our base will be unstable. I know it because I have been on both sides of that coin. When my self-image is healthy, I can withstand the inevitable challenges in life without self-destructing.

I titled this chapter 'Laughing' because nothing was better than being with my Dad when he was laughing with abandon. If you were fortunate to witness his laughter, then you know what I am talking about. It was so contagious. On many occasions, I would find myself laughing just because of his laughter. It was a joyous thing to experience.

Dad's remedy for not feeling good, mentally or physically, was to take some time and watch a good comedy. He thought that if you could find something to laugh at, the vibration you are in would change.

My father would look for the humor in any situation. He knew there was always two sides (and often more) to everything. By finding humor, he never got overwhelmed. And that attitude calmed all of us and made the rough patches easier.

Seeing the good and finding the laughter is a great strategy to conduct your life by.

You may have heard Bob Proctor tell the following story from the stage. It brought humor to a painful experience in his life, and he laughed that deep laugh every time he told it.

As you learned in an earlier chapter, my father adored his mother. When my Nan was in the hospital and close to passing away, the family took turns being there for support.

At one point, when Dad was at Nan's bedside, a nurse told him that when a patient is close to death, sometimes they need permission from those they love most and that the way to do that is to say to them that it is okay to go. So, she suggested that Dad give permission to Nan to die. She said it would make it easier for her to let go.

Nan had been in a progressive decline; she had not responded for several days. Finally, Dad stood up, leaned over, and whispered in her ear, "Mother, it's okay to go."

Her eyes popped open, and she looked wide-eyed at my father and said, "Where are we going?" It scared the heck out of him because he wasn't expecting a response.

Where their conversation went from there, I don't know. But I will never forget his hearty laughter when telling this story. He found humor and made a sad moment more bearable.

I love that memory of Dad on stage kissing himself. I love how it incited laughter in a big room with hundreds of people.

When I feel sad about my father not being here with me physically, I close my eyes and hear his laughter. Sometimes I will happen upon a video of his on YouTube and hear that joy in his voice. It fills me with warmth and changes the vibration of my body.

My granddaughter Nora watching her great grandpa on YouTube

CONSIDER...

Try abandoning yourself to
joy and pure laughter.

Pain and discomfort take a backseat in our thoughts when we let go. Laughter doesn't erase pain but makes it a little easier to bear.

Have you ever listened to a
child's laughter? Like my Dad,
their joy is infectious.

A fun exercise for kids is creating a 'Feel Good Box.' If you have young children, I encourage you to try this and do it with them. First, decorate a shoe box together, and then the two of you fill it with special mementos and perhaps pictures that make the child smile or laugh. Then, on bad days, sit together with the box and go through it. It is an excellent opportunity to teach a child about shifting their vibration, and laughter is great medicine.

The 'Feel Good Box' exercise can extend beyond kids. Make one for yourself! I use a glass box that I keep on my desk. It is filled with small items and photos that bring me joy.

Self-image sprouts from self-love.

If this is an area you need to work on, make it a priority. Right now.

NOTES:

Let It Go

*"Let us not look back in anger
nor forward in fear,
but around us in awareness."*
— Leland 'Val' Van De Wall

Do you ever replay old stories in your mind? Unfortunately, more often than not, the stories we play on repeat do not move us forward; they hold us back.

If you are finding your thoughts are looping and are intrusive, working to let that go is its own special kind of freedom.

Our thoughts and stories are very real to us; they are our perceptions that include data from our past, present, and future. And if intrusive, those thoughts can keep us from moving forward into growth.

I grew up hearing my Dad say, "Whatever's happened in the past is in the past. The only place the past exists is in your mind. It is no longer happening to you right now. So, don't keep it alive if it is not serving you."

"Brian, let it go!" was at the top of Dad's toolkit when I was growing up. He would listen when I said I needed to talk, and then he would ask me if what I was telling him was making my life better. Of course, it usually wasn't, and he would simply say, "Let it go." I remember being frustrated with this when I was young, but as an adult, I appreciate the simplicity of this message. I often just say to myself, "That's right, Brian – let it go. Don't try to complicate this. Make space for the good."

The opportunity in letting go is identifying what is mentally and emotionally draining you. Then, by letting it go, you create a new empty space that can be filled by conscious choice.

I have noticed in my own family how a shared experience gets molded into a memory or story to fit our chosen role. We use our stories to form our identities. We use them as evidence to support the person we are today. And, sometimes, we trap ourselves in a thought loop we can't escape.

My parents divorced when I was 14 years old. I have a younger sister and a younger brother – so the three of us each have slightly different memories and stories of our parent's divorce. Nevertheless, each of our stories support our point of view about that event and how we define ourselves today.

We each are biased by our own perspective that is further narrowed by our ages at the time and the story molding that happens through hearing others tell it. Additionally, these memories are also shaped by how we saw our place in that event, as well as the present-day role we now occupy in life.

For each of us, our stories are correct, even if they are different.

My way of thinking was formed by growing up with Bob Proctor and working directly next to him for close to 30 years of our 60 years together. That experience leads me to hold onto more positive memories… and, more importantly, to let go of negative thoughts. I have learned to give very little energy to the struggles I endured. I know this is because of how I was raised. I know it is from watching my Dad and paying attention as a young child.

Before Cory and I were married, Dad created an affirmation that she continues to use today. You see, Cory has perfectionist tendencies; she can get stuck in details and have difficulty moving forward. This affirmation helped her so much that she pulled the word *LET* out of it and wrote it everywhere with a dry-erase marker.

LET was on her car windshield, it was on her bathroom mirror, and it was written across her kitchen window – all places she would see multiple times a day. It was her reminder to 'Let Go.'

What seeing the word *LET* did for Cory was cue her to pause, and make space, by letting go of the thought she was ruminating over; this helped her to move forward.

At events, my father would bring Cory on stage to recite the affirmation, and that is when he got the idea of how to help others with it.

In 2018 Dad had our graphic designer create an artistic rendition of the word *LET*. It was beautiful and calming to look at. He then had thousands of copies made and laminated, and we gave them away at events. He would instruct people to place this placard somewhere they would see throughout the day.

My father knew that the most important conversations we have are the ones we have with ourselves, and that life is really an invisible power that flows to and through us. If life is feeling flat, then we should look for where the resistance is. Of course, it is in our thoughts. So, examine your thoughts - the chatter that plays on a loop in your mind. If that chatter is intrusive and has become an obstacle to your growth, do the work to deal with it.

With intention, you can lessen the emotional burden of the resistance, and when you do this, you will create room for the good you desire to flow to and through you.

An exercise I have used to lessen the emotional burden is to identify the intrusive thoughts and then allow myself to engage differently with that memory to gain a new perspective. I look inward and edit that story – literally. I do this by writing it out on paper in detail. Doing this helps me to release the emotional weight and makes space for moving on.

Finally, I look for the good that has resulted. It may not feel equal to the pain, but there is always good.

Cory's affirmation: *"I am so happy and grateful now that I LET everything in my life flow free and easy, and I focus only on what serves me toward my greater good."*

Let

I am so happy and grateful now that
I LET everything in my life flow free and easy,
and I focus only on what serves me
toward my greater good.

Dad with his wife Linda

CONSIDER...

If you are held captive by the stories you are telling yourself, rewrite the story.

When we are ready to create meaningful change, we can take the step to consciously differentiate between what makes us feel good and what makes us feel flawed or inadequate. Suspend any judgment you have put on yourself and ask yourself the question, "How is this story serving me?"

Examine your thoughts.

Are they keeping you stuck in a place that has become your comfort zone? All memories carry associated emotions. However, some are connected to strong negative emotions and tend to be the ones that take up the most real estate in our mind. Start by finding a way to both honor your feelings and to forgive; maybe it is forgiving yourself. This is critical. If you do not forgive, your energy will be stuck and your creative power restricted.

Try being proactive in changing your perspective rather than being passive.

Start to notice how much of your creative energy you anchor in the past with attached shame, guilt, or blame. These are emotions that keep us stuck. Write it all out. Writing causes thinking and engages our mind differently. That single word, LET, can serve as a reminder to quickly move on from any thoughts blocking our energy when that looping chatter begins.

You have the ability within you to set yourself free.

261

NOTES:

Cory's son, Spencer, with Dad

CHAPTER 11

SUCCESS

The Power Of A Vision Board

*"There is a difference between wishing
for a thing and being ready to receive it."
- Bob Proctor*

I've always loved hearing this quote spoken by my father. The quote was originally written by Napoleon Hill. I often refer to it when striving to reach my biggest goals. Here it is in its entirety:

> *"There is a difference between wishing for a thing and being ready to receive it. No one is ready for a thing, until he believes he can acquire it. The state of mind must be belief, not mere hope or wish. Open-mindedness is essential for belief."*

The reason I resonate with this quote is that it lines up with one of my favorite goal achieving tools – the vision board.

There is no denying the power of the visual aspect – what the eyes see, the mind believes. I've found that it's best to use every tool possible when building an image in my subconscious mind of exactly how I want to live. And the vision board is a physical representation of what you are impressing on your subconscious mind.

I begin by gathering pictures that represent how I want to live my life. These pictures may be for material items like a boat and symbolic things like a sunset on a beach I want to visit. I always include images that, to me, convey healthy relationships. This can consist of romance, friendship, parenting, or really anything. I have included pictures of what I would like our home to look like, how it would appear when completely renovated, and its location. I have also used images of a healthy and fit body, cars that I like, and other things that motivate me. And I use images that evoke emotion within me.

Because of the emotional connection that forms when you take a photo, use those when you can. For example, if a specific car is what you desire, go to the showroom and take a picture of that particular car with you sitting in it. Find one in the color you want, and as you take the photo, imagine yourself as the owner and what that will feel like. Make a mental note of that new-car smell. Register in your memory the sound of the engine.

Now, whenever you look at that photo on your vision board, you will feel the emotion you held when taking it. You will remember going there to take the picture and the fun you had doing it. You are creating emotion around your desire.

I like to frame my vision board collage and hang it on our

bedroom wall like a piece of art. This way, it is what I see first thing when I wake up and the last thing at the end of the day.

When I look at my vision board, I let my body feel the emotion of a deep knowing – that I am ready to receive and I will accomplish everything on my board easily.

My stepson, Spencer, recently shared a funny story about vision boards.

A few years ago, when Spencer was in college for engineering, he had a roommate Tyler, who was a business major. A project Tyler was given in a class was to create a vision board.

At the time, Spencer thought it was childish and a waste of time. He felt buried in his engineering classes, while his roommate majoring in business, was cutting out pictures and pasting them on a poster board. Spencer and I laugh about it now because he has come to clearly understand the value and significance of vision boards in building the future he wants.

When conducting seminars in Los Angeles, my wife Cory would invite Spencer to attend. At the time, he was living in San Luis Obispo (not far from LA) and attending school. Spencer always declined, saying he was too busy. Finally, his roommate Tyler talked him into attending and asked if he could come along.

When we told Dad that Spencer and Tyler were coming he made space for them at the front and center table, where he could clearly see them and make eye contact. At the first break, Dad came over to Cory and I and asked, "Did you see those kids? Spencer has not stopped taking notes."

At the end of the day, we had dinner with the boys, and Spencer showed us all his notes. He excitedly explained, "This stuff is real; this is exactly what I am studying at university. It's just that it is wrapped up in science talk at school, but the concepts are the same."

At that moment, Spencer harnessed the power of my father's work; you could see the wheels in his mind turning. And when he combined the material with his education, he very quickly put himself on the fast track to goal achievement. He has gone after and achieved one goal after another since that first seminar, with the vision board now playing a large role in his life.

Spencer and Tyler both have become great students of my father. They attended many of our seminars and workshops in Los Angeles and even came to Toronto together to attend our Matrixx event. It was at that event that they created a business together.

It was beautiful to watch how being in the energy of that room and spending time with my father expanded their thinking. You could literally see it happening. It was also during that event that Dad surprised the boys by asking them to meet him in one of the rooms one morning before the day got started.

Dad had brought his tailor to the hotel and had both Spencer and Tyler measured for custom suits. That is a moment those two will never forget. And both these boys have become regular suit wearers; they have made it a part of their self-image – and I know that is because of my father.

Cory and I recently returned from a short trip to Chicago to attend Tyler's wedding. I don't know if he had a special woman on his vision board, but we could tell instantly that he married someone who compliments who he is. Spencer was in the wedding party, and it was an absolute joy for Cory and I to witness where these two young men are now.

Also, knowing what the seminars and my Dad's teaching did for them both brings us incredible satisfaction.

CONSIDER...

**First, you must ask yourself,
"Am I ready to receive?"**

If you have yet to do that work, you will be out of alignment with the vision board exercise. You must know you are worthy of receiving.

**Take some time over the next week
and think about what you would
like your life to look and feel like.**

Don't worry about what anyone else thinks. Instead, ask yourself the question – "What do I want?" What kind of experiences and physical things would you like to have in your life? What kind of relationships would you like to have?

What good would you like to share with the world? Begin by finding pictures in magazines or online that anchor those thoughts and desires in your mind, images that stir emotions within you.

Next, get a nice picture frame or poster board and put the pictures all together in a way that feels good to you. As I mentioned, I put mine on my bedroom wall in full view. Do whatever works, but please do it. At first, it may seem a bit silly, but in time you will see it working. In fact, just the act of creating the board will cause a shift in your energy. Pay attention to that shift.

Every image I have kept on my vision board has shown up in my life. I may have removed an idea because my desires changed, but I have never removed one because it wasn't realized. Ever.

To wrap this up, I will return to the question asked at the beginning because for this to work, you must be ready to receive.

Ask yourself, "Do I willingly give?" and "Am I ready to receive?" Giving and receiving are different expressions of the same flow of energy; to work, they must work together.

NOTES:

The Rewards Of A Vision

" Thoughts become things.
If you can see it in your mind,
you will hold it in your hand."
— Bob Proctor

In November 2016, my father was to be honored at Carnegie Hall in New York City for his long-time work in personal development, and I wouldn't have missed it for the world. I immediately booked my travel and flew in two days ahead of the event to take in all the city has to offer.

I had another motive for arriving early. I enjoy old collector cars, and I knew of a specific showroom in the heart of New York City. This showroom has a reputation for featuring the finest there is to offer in collectible cars and for selling these old cars in concourse condition, which means that when a car is sold from there, it is as good as the day it rolled out of the factory.

My dream car has always been an Austin Healey 3000. It's a car that has been on my vision board for many years. So, on my first day in New York, I got up early and took a long walk, and found my way to the showroom in Greenwich Village.

When I arrived at the showroom late on my first morning in New York, the doors were locked, and the lights were out. Normally,

I would have turned around and left. However, I knew having this opportunity and standing in front of this door after so many years of having an Austin Healey on my vision board meant something to me, so I stayed.

There was a small intercom button on the outside wall next to the door; I rang it to see if I would get an answer.

To my surprise, someone answered immediately and said they were closed and that the showroom was an appointment-only location. I told him that I'd been following the site online and that I was only in town for a few days. I then said that I was very interested in seeing what they had. He asked me to wait, saying I was lucky to have caught him because it was his day off, and he had just stopped by to check something. He said, "I'll be right down to open the door."

As I waited, I could see several cars through the window. I saw old Porsches, Ferraris, Jaguars, and other vehicles. Every one of them looked pristine.

Then, the lights came on, and a young man came to the door and let me in. He introduced himself as Kyle. As soon as I walked into the showroom, my eyes landed on an Austin Healey 3000, exactly like what I had on my vision board. As I walked straight to it, I told Kyle I had been looking for one of these for many years; however, the hassle of restoring one had held me back. This car I was staring down at was perfect! And I mean perfect as if it had just rolled off the assembly line.

Now, the funny thing is, I had never even sat in an Austin Healey before. I had seen a few at car shows and always loved how they looked and sounded, but this was the first time I had the opportunity to actually sit in one. It felt incredible, and immediately I was able to see myself driving around Florida with the top down and the sunshine on my face, just as I had imagined so many times before. I knew this was the one.

The car was a perfect 1962 model, it felt and looked like it was new. It was as if I'd been transported back in time. The color was a gorgeous ivory white with black coves and wire wheels. Kyle opened the hood, and inside stood a motor so clean that you could eat off it.

I sat in that car and let myself feel what it would be like to own it. I walked slowly around the car and took in the clean lines and its beauty. This was exactly what I had been visioning for years.

But as soon as we got into talking about the price, I instantly got uncomfortable. I felt sick.

I kept a good poker face, but in my head, all I could hear was a low buzz. Finally, in a calm voice, I said it was far more than I was prepared to pay and said I needed time to give it some thought. I took several pictures from every angle and then walked out the door, saying I would be in touch with him later.

I was vibrating as I started the long walk back to my hotel. I felt like this car was meant for me. That moment when what you've imagined manifests in physical form is surreal, and that is exactly how I felt: like this was all a dream.

As it just so happened, I was only a month shy of turning 55. Since I was young, the number 55 has been my favorite number. No significant reason; I just liked how the number looked and sounded. And 55 became the number I chose for everything, including sports. So in my mind, I considered this a special birthday, and I wanted my 55th birthday to be meaningful; I wanted to mark my 55th year in a way that I would never forget.

As my birthday approached, I had yet to come up with anything that would make this birthday different. So that day as I was walking back to the hotel, I began thinking… what if I bought this car as a birthday gift to myself?

That would certainly be something that would make it unforgettable.

The trouble was – my paradigm. I was having a battle in my head over the asking price. In my mind, I was listing all my commitments and obligations for which I needed my cash reserves, and buying a car that would only be driven occasionally felt like a luxury I couldn't really afford.

At that moment, I did the one thing I knew would make me uncomfortable and send me through the Terror Barrier. I sent pictures of the car to my Dad and called him. He was the master at getting me to stretch way outside my comfort zone.

As I spoke to him and told him what a unique car this was, he said, "Then you should go back and buy it."

I started listing all the reasons why I shouldn't do that, and then I said the one thing that put me across the line. I told Dad that I thought it would be a good thing to buy as a birthday present to myself so that I would never forget my 55th birthday. That was all I needed to say.

In no uncertain terms, my father told me that I needed to stretch and find a way to make it work. He convinced me I deserved to treat myself well, and then he went on to talk about how most people have trouble treating themselves well and what a mistake that is. That was all I needed to hear.

I called Kyle and said I would like to come back and negotiate a fair deal for the car.

When I arrived, the lights were on, and Kyle was ready to unlock the door and let me back in. We started to discuss the price, and he had the company owner get on a call with me. We talked for a few minutes and agreed on a price. Then, still feeling quite uncomfortable and sick to my stomach, I heard myself say, "I'm in." It was like an out-of-body experience with my paradigm screaming in my ear, "You can't do this!"

We went upstairs into the office and began writing up the agreement and discussing how the car would be shipped to my home in Florida.

Afterward, as I was walking back to the hotel feeling both terrified and excited, I called Kyle and asked if he could please email me the British Heritage Certificate on the car. He said he would do it right away and that I would have it by the time I returned to my room.

As I mentioned, the car was a 1962 model. I was born on December 8, 1961. When I received the email from Kyle and looked at the certificate, I nearly fell over. This car I had just purchased had begun production on December 8, 1961 — the day I was born!

You can't make this kind of thing up! Call it what you will; I know I attracted this to me. It really drove home the impact of a vision board and how it assists you with getting onto a specific vibrational frequency. I had spent years looking at a picture of this car, so having this happen was just a natural conclusion to the idea that had been my dream and on my vision board.

What I love most about this story is that Dad never projected his personal thoughts about this purchase onto me. He was not remotely into collector cars and would have never done anything like this. He could have easily said to me, "Brian, that's crazy! Why would you want something like that?" It would have been very easy for him to squash my dream.

Instead, he supported me; it brought him joy to see the joy it brought me. He encouraged me and took pleasure in seeing me treat myself well.

Now, a car is just a simple example. Dad would support and encourage me toward anything that I wanted for my life. That constant support shaped my life. I always felt like I had his hand on my back.

I can hear my father's voice flowing through me now when I encourage my kids to do whatever it takes to follow their dreams. Even when what they want makes no sense to me whatsoever, I can see it means something to them. Because of my experience, I know how my encouragement makes them feel, and it is a feeling of unconditional love.

CONSIDER...

Think of a time in your life when you manifested something, someone, or a situation.

Write it out in detail. Then, include all the emotions that go along with that experience.

Think of something you would like to manifest now.

Now build your vision board with images that support your desires. Act as if you have already manifested your desire. Go to car showrooms. Attend open houses. Go out on dates. Meet your desires with action.

Write it out.

The images you use for your vision board should also be a part of your big goal that you write out in detail. Write it often and read it daily. The simple act of writing things down dramatically increases the likelihood of your words turning into action.

"What the hand does, the mind remembers." – Madame Montessori

NOTES:

Powerful Life Script

I want to share a tool for your toolbox that aligns with the vision board and writing out your goal. My friend, Peggy McColl, calls this tool the *Power Life Script®*. She has been using it for years and watching her results convinced me to start doing it too.

It began with Peggy writing the details of her dream life that included all she wanted to accomplish, as if it had already happened. Then, she read aloud what she wrote and recorded it. She would then listen to her recording several times a day. And eventually, she named it The Power Life Script®, and she even trademarked the process and turned it into an online course.

I watched Peggy consistently grow and do things in her business and personal life that kept taking her to the next level. When she drew the line from the recording she'd made to her recent results, I got busy and did my own.

My father taught me that repetition is essential if you want to change something in your life for the better. I realized that this was precisely what Peggy was doing. She had created something she could listen to repeatedly that would change her way of thinking.

When I created a recording for myself, I first built a mental image of my big picture and then wrote it out. It included my beautiful marriage, the kind of income I was earning, and how I was active and healthy. I talked about our kids and how they were thriving.

I covered every part of my life and worded it in the present tense as if it was already here.

After I recorded it, I started to listen to it regularly. It was good, but for me, the sound of my own voice was off-putting and distracting. It made it hard for me to emotionally connect with the recording.

Then, I had one of those "AHA" moments. My wife Cory has been a godsend to me. She has changed so many things in my life for the better. And something that has always struck me about her is her voice. To me, she has the most beautiful voice I have ever heard. I love listening to her talk.

When we are driving long distances together, Cory often reads out loud to me. It was on one of those drives when she was reading to me that I got the thought...

"What if I have Cory read and record my life script for me?"

She recorded it for me in a way that felt like we were having a conversation. She told me how proud she is of all I had accomplished. She then discussed all the good that I have created in my life. Essentially, she just took my life script and read it to me as if whispering in my ear about all the goals I have hit, the difference I have made and how fulfilling our life together is.

Every morning, I listen to this recording of my wife talking directly to me. My life script, read by Cory, has resonated so strongly with me that I absolutely love listening to it. And I feel her words when she speaks.

Taking this one extra step really changed what this recording does for me. As I write this, I realize that what Cory recorded for me was over two years ago. Yet, almost every morning, I have listened to it, and nearly everything in that recording has already become a reality. It is absolute magic.

Now it is time for me to create a new script that is even bigger and better and ask her to record it for me once more. Again, this tool is a simple and meaningful way to speak to my subconscious mind, and you can use it too.

A funny side note to this story is that when Peggy heard that I had Cory record my script, she thought that was a great idea and wrote out her script as if her husband Denis was reading it to her.

She then asked Denis to read it while they recorded it together. Reading the script was the first-time Denis had heard Peggy's big goals. When he read some of the income goals Peggy wanted for herself, his voice would rise, and he excitedly laughed and became animated. This was so much fun for Peggy that she kept the recording just as it was. It gave her another level of emotion that she connected with, and she ended up listening to it more often.

I can tell you from personal experience that taking the time to think about your future, and then writing out in detail what your future is – how it looks and feels to you – and then recording and listening to it daily or multiple times a day is an exercise worth doing. This is a tool available to you right now without cost.

As I was writing this chapter, I remembered an article Dad would often recommend that had helped him over the years. The writing was titled, *The Common Denominator of Success by Albert E.N. Gray*. Essentially, it distills the simple truth behind what makes people successful or average. It has nothing to do with intellect, money, education, or any of the things we might naturally attribute to success. Instead, the author proposed that:

"Success comes from the habit of doing things that failures don't like to do."

Success is simple but not easy. It is not easy because people too easily give up, especially when they don't see instant results. However, you can choose to be different from the masses because following the masses is almost always a mistake. Thinking about and talking about doing something is very different from taking action.

CONSIDER...

Will you take committed action
and do this exercise?

NOTES:

He Wanted The Sweater

" If you know what to do to reach your goal,
it's not a big enough goal."
— Bob Proctor

Maybe like me, you have been a student of Bob Proctor for as long as you can remember, and you have heard him share his story of feeling lost in life until the age of 27 when he was given the book *Think and Grow Rich by Napoleon Hill*.

Because I have only known my Dad as a student of the material he taught, I've often thought... there must have been something special in him as a child. Yet, he never talked like there was.

Until I heard... The Yo-Yo Story.

I can still clearly see and hear Dad on stage telling this story at seminars as he'd pull a Cheerio Yo-Yo from his suit pocket. It would surprise everyone, including us (his support team). This was part of what made my Dad fun. I cannot think of anyone else in the industry who captured an audience's attention quite like him.

Dad would start by saying that to grow, we must stretch our goals beyond the reach of our current understanding. He would then ask the audience if anyone knew how to play a Yo-Yo. Inevitably there would always be hands that would go up.

This story began when my father was 13 and at a public school in the Beaches neighborhood of Toronto. There was a boy older than my Dad who walked the Beaches neighborhood streets with a level of confidence that captivated young Bob Proctor.

Every day after school, Dad would search the neighborhood to see if he could find this boy; his name was Ricky McGinnis. Ricky worked for the Cheerio Yo-Yo company in Canada. He was a Yo-Yo Champion and became the Cheerio Yo-Yo brand ambassador. Ricky would work in different neighborhoods to entice the kids to play with a Yo-Yo and subsequently increase sales for the company.

When Ricky walked around the neighborhood, he always wore a maroon V-neck sleeveless sweater with a prominent crest of the Cheerio logo emblazoned across the front center of his chest with the words Yo-Yo Champion. In addition, his sweater had little badges sewn all over, signifying different tricks that Ricky had mastered.

Because it was easy to break strings when working on mastering certain tricks, Ricky carried dozens of replacement strings around his neck. At the time, it cost a nickel to buy two Yo-Yo strings; that was a lot of money in those days for a child. However, if you could master a trick in front of Ricky, he would give you a couple of his strings.

Ricky was like the pied piper. He had all the kids following him, and my father was one of them. Ricky would teach Dad and others new tricks as they walked the neighborhood together. Eventually, he would test them on the trick.

At this point, while telling the story, Dad would start to play with the Yo-Yo on stage. And it was always a Cheerio Yo-Yo.

He talked about how he remembered some of the tricks, and then he'd do them on stage. First, he would show the audience tricks such as the *Sleeper, Walk the Dog, Shoot the Moon, and Rock the Baby.* Then, he would end it with a trick called *Bite the Dog* and joke that it often did. This would get a huge laugh as Dad would throw the Yo-Yo down between his legs, and it would jump up and grab onto the back of his pants. You could almost hear the men in the audience gasp when he did this trick.

While showing the tricks on stage, Dad would talk about Ricky and how Ricky had come up with an idea that got my Dad's attention.

You see, one day, Ricky surprised the young group with a competition that he'd put together for them. The winner would get a sweater, just like Ricky's. To win, you had to be able to do all the regular tricks, along with a really difficult one called *The Brain Twister.*

Dad would talk about how he remembers getting emotionally involved with the idea of wearing that sweater and walking around town with it on. He talked about how he imagined all the pretty girls whispering, "That's him. He's the boy who won the sweater." Even on stage, you could feel him reliving the experience and how special he felt.

Young Bob was committed to the idea of winning that sweater. Dad shared with me later that, in hindsight, this was his first recollection of setting a goal... of wanting something so much that he was emotionally involved with the image of wearing that sweater and could feel what it would be like. He was practicing the power of visualization before he really knew what it was.

Then on stage, as a man well into his 80's, he would perform the difficult trick called *The Brain Twister*, like he'd been doing it his whole life. Every time he did this, the audience was completely still. The trick usually drew a standing ovation!

Bob Proctor whipping out a Yo-Yo and performing mind-blowing tricks was the last thing anyone expected to witness. Then, he would invite people in the audience who thought they could do that trick to come on stage with him. As you can imagine, no one did.

He would laugh and say, "What about those of you who raised your hand when I asked who could play the Yo-Yo?"

He then went on to say, "The reason I won the sweater was because of how attached I was to the idea of winning it and wearing it. And the others couldn't do that trick because they didn't want the sweater."

As cute as it was, that statement was the lesson. He would follow that up with, "What is your sweater? What is it that you really want?"

In order to get that sweater, Dad had to practice a lot. He became obsessed with the idea of wearing the sweater. His practice was mental and emotional as well as physical.

He was so committed to his goal that he changed his daily schedule to make time for the work required to win. Instead of playing with friends after school, he went straight home to practice. And some of the tricks were painful to learn. If the Yo-Yo was not thrown down hard enough, it would pop back and hit him on the knuckles, leaving marks. He would also break strings and have to use all his allowance to replace them rather than go to the movies with friends.

He had built the picture of what he wanted, was committed to the outcome, and did the work.

My father won that sweater, and he proudly wore it everywhere. But more importantly, he learned the valuable lesson of setting a goal and going after it.

Later, once he figured out what he wanted for his life, this first lesson reminded him of the discipline it would take to get there. And discipline is a skill that can be learned. We are all capable of it.

CONSIDER...

What are you willing to do for your goal?
Are you prepared to commit to
doing the work to achieve it?
What are you prepared to sacrifice?

These are the questions we all must ask when going after big goals. What's important when you are going after something you've never achieved before is who you become in the process of reaching the goal. This is part of the divine plan for you as a spiritual being. My father would say, "The purpose of a goal is not to GET – it is to GROW."

Also, my Dad shared a very powerful definition of the word sacrifice: "Giving up something of a lower nature for something of a higher nature." Many people think of sacrifice as a negative thing, but using this definition, it's incredibly powerful. For example, you can give up a disempowering belief for a supportive one, or you can give up binge-watching Netflix each night and instead using that time to study and hone your skills.

Goals are essential to living
a creative life.

Every expression of life is constantly moving in one direction or another. Either you are improving the quality of your life, or you are reducing it.

What are you hungry for?

NOTES:

What Do You Want?

*"All things are possible if
the motivation is strong enough."*
— Bob Proctor

When I was in my 20's and starting to work as a real estate agent, I loved to attend my father's goal-achieving seminars. Of course, I knew the importance of having a goal, but that particular seminar always lit a fire within me. It was the exercise Dad had us do to figure out what we wanted. Following that event, my sales would consistently skyrocket!

Dad instructed us all to take a piece of paper and write down what we would like to be, do, and have. Now, the key here was never to think about how you would achieve it. Instead, he said to write as if you had a magic wand and could make anything appear. Anything. It didn't matter how crazy your desires felt. Just write it out.

That's it! Simple, right?

I quickly discovered that it wasn't simple; immediately, I was getting in my own way. I remember writing things that felt ridiculous, and my paradigm would immediately kick in, telling me I wasn't worthy of the big things. I was also embarrassed, even though I was the only one seeing what I was writing. However, Dad clearly said we had to open our mind and write without judgement, whatever our hearts desired. This is what I mean when I say it wasn't simple. I had to fight these feelings and keep on writing. And the success I experienced each time I attended Dad's goal-achieving seminars was because I pushed through that discomfort and did the exercise as it was laid out. I didn't cut corners. I know it helped that I could quickly identify that the walls I was hitting were indeed my paradigm and not absolute.

Because this exercise was more challenging for me than I thought it should be, let me ask you... What do you want?

Most people have not been raised to consider what they truly want for their life. Most people go from point A to point B and so on by default. Either they are doing what someone else wants for them, or they are making choices to make someone else happy.

Fortunately, I grew up with Bob Proctor. But that still didn't make this exercise easy. Discovering what you really want begins with letting your imagination run wild and then deciding to go after whatever that is – if it inspires you.

Deciding what we want and staying focused on that vision is the biggest hurdle most of us face. I have many memories of setting big goals with Dad looking over my shoulder and encouraging me to step it up a notch.

It wasn't until later in life that I realized it wasn't because of the big things I was going after that he was so interested. Instead, it was because of the growth I would experience along the way by stretching myself in pursuit of the big things.

Dad had created three categories for goals that he used when teaching:

A-type goal:
This is a goal that you already *know* how to do.

B- type goal:
Something that is a stretch, but you *think* you can do it.

C-type goal:
A goal that you really want... something that truly inspires you, but it scares you at the same time.
You also have no idea how to achieve it!

He said there is no long-lasting inspiration in doing something you already know how to achieve; and that it is essential to go after a C-type goal because that is where growth happens; it happens in the stretching. Going after something that really fires you up causes you to do things in a day you would normally never do, perhaps even in a lifetime. These are the kind of goals that not only excite you but can also terrify you.

The other important factor is not sharing your goal with people who won't support you, especially in the beginning when you can easily be knocked down because you are still building confidence around your ideas. When you start to go after C-type goals, people in your life will notice something different about you. They will see you doing things that cause you to stand out. This is when you need to have strength. You need to keep moving forward even if you feel judged. Most of the time, others want you to stay in their comfort zone of how they see you. This is not because they don't care for you; it's because they are resisting change.

I have achieved some incredible things in my life, and it wasn't always comfortable. My father encouraged me to get uncomfortable, and he was always there to cheer me on. He'd say, "Uncomfortable is good, Bri." And because of him and his teachings, I am living a far more rewarding life than I imagined.

The goal line for what I can achieve is always moving because of my belief in this process and my faith in myself.

I don't care to give energy to the negative. That is not to say that I don't have negativity in my life; I just choose not to provide it with energy.

A few years back, we held a seminar in Toronto filled with people from all over the world looking to improve their life and business. When I worked with this group on solutions and strategies, I found the method to creating winning results relatively simple, but I also acknowledged that it can be challenging to follow.

The method was to be fully present in the moment and to do the best you can in that moment. Then move on to the next moment, the next hour, the next day, and so on.

Too many of us look at our past, hang on to it, and let it define who we are. We cannot change it. Good or bad, our history is what it is. If I ever complained about a past wrong, Dad would say to me, "You can't change the time you got out of bed this morning." His words remind me that right now is the moment we can influence.

Dad was a master at achieving big things. He just knew in his heart he was going to achieve whatever it was he went after, and he only surrounded himself with people who saw that in him as well.

If you want the good life, you need to have an image of what that is for you and plant that image in the soil of your subconscious mind. The moment you do, your vibration will change. And at this higher vibration (frequency) of living, you will attract what you are in harmony with — as surely as it's going to get dark tonight.

If you stay focused on doing the best you can in the current day, minute or moment, and with your big, beautiful vision planted in your subconscious mind... you will recognize new opportunities that align with your thoughts. Keep your eyes, mind and heart wide open.

Just a few days before my father passed, I was sitting in the ICU of the hospital with him. Even during this time when he was not well, he was asking me about my goals and what I was going after. He had a big smile on his face and was so happy. Dad could see that I was going after big things that might not make sense to most people. He knew that I understood the assignment he'd been teaching me for sixty years.

CONSIDER...

Your goal must be something you seriously want; Something you won't lose interest in at the first challenge.

As Zig Ziglar said, "A goal that is casually set and lightly taken is freely abandoned at the first obstacle."

To discover what you really want, begin by believing in make-believe. Tap into your imagination and spend time with a pen and paper and write down whatever comes to your mind about how you want to live, and what you would like your relationships and life experiences to be like. Everything you'd like to be, do and have. Then, take what you have written, add a lot of detail, make your vision grand and fun, and build it into something worth trading your life for. We trade our life for something anyway; we should make that trade worthwhile.

I encourage you to do this exercise, and if you have kids, have them do it too. Pay attention to what makes your heart quicken. This is a great way to figure out what truly inspires you.

NOTES:

Quantum Leap

"Most people confuse wishing and wanting with pursuing. You must place your trust in __action__."
— Price Pritchett

Dad was often asked about his top 5 books. And, of course, his number one was always *Think and Grow Rich by Napoleon Hill*. Let's face it – that was the book that changed the course of his life, and that is the one he always had in his possession. In fact, that book was so well-read that it was falling apart. He had a wide rubber band wrapped around it to hold it together, and a pouch to store it in when he traveled.

Many people over the years tried to give him a new edition or have the old one repaired. He would never consider doing that. In his eyes, the book that he had held in his hands since October 1961 was an old friend that carried the energy of his journey, and he would never part with it or change it. Today when I hold that book in my hands, I can feel my father's energy.

Another book at the top of Dad's list was *You²* by *Price Pritchett*, who you met in the Foreword of this book.

You², aka *"You Squared"*, is a quantum leap manual. At just 36 pages in length, it's a booklet more than a book. But Dad would say, "Don't let that fool you. Those 36 pages contain some of the most powerful lessons I have ever learned."

When Dad first picked up *You²*, he immediately resonated with the story and the concepts laid out by Price. He recognized himself in the book and realized he'd made many quantum leaps throughout his life. He could connect the dots.

You² is a thesis in not settling and, instead, imagining breakthroughs in achievement that are not incremental or gradual; instead they are both dramatic and huge – a quantum leap.

It is a formula for a different kind of route to success.

When teaching on stage, Dad would hold up *You²* and say, "You should get a copy." Price Pritchett, the book's author, got wind of Bob Proctor promoting his book from the stage and phoned my father, asking what he was doing – because his book sales were skyrocketing. Well, this sparked a friendship between them that lasted many years.

I was fortunate to have met Price in person. Dad and I had dinner with him one night after a seminar in Los Angeles. I was struck by how kind and incredibly thoughtful Price is in his thinking.

After meeting and hearing him speak, I understood why Dad respected Price so much. It was a treat to watch the two of them interact. Price is from Texas; he has a warm southern drawl and a way of speaking that puts you at ease. They were like old friends, really enjoying each other's company.

During dinner, Price talked about quantum leaps. But what really stuck with me was when he said that most people tend to advance in life at a measured pace – essentially moving up in life a single step at a time.

His theory was that anyone could make an explosive jump and move multiple steps simultaneously, seemingly at odds with common sense and without apparent effort. He continued by saying that what it required was a change in habits.

Price said, "If you want to accelerate your achievement rate rapidly, you must search out and vigorously employ new behaviors."

When he said that, I realized why my father was as successful as he was. He was constantly (with intention) doing things that changed his behaviors, which changed his habits. And it was the little things he did that added up and caused the quantum leaps in his life. For example, Dad told me that every morning he would write out a statement or way of thinking multiple times to 'anchor' it in his mind. By doing this, he was convincing his subconscious mind that it was so.

When you first hear the idea of a quantum leap, it can seem ridiculous and impossible. However, when you make a big jump forward and look back, it always seems more straight forward than when you started.

As Price said, quantum leaps occur when there is a radical departure from our routine habits. To make a change – you must do something different, which takes conscious effort. You have to exercise conscious control to bring yourself back to the new (desired) behavior over and over until it has become a habit.

At our Paradigm Shift event, Dad would give a simple exercise designed to do this. The practice demonstrated the discipline it will take to create a new habit and show how making a change – even on a small scale – will be uncomfortable at first.

The exercise was to write out an affirmation in a clean journal that you use only for this purpose. You write the affirmation once with your dominant hand, and then ten times daily for thirty days you write it out using your non-dominant hand. This may only make sense to you once you try it, but you will have real and lasting breakthroughs by committing to this.

I can say this because I have personally done it, and I have witnessed the breakthroughs in others. The exercise is forging new pathways that will serve you when you apply the same tenacity to other real changes you want to make in your life.

Gradually, you will see the way to what you are imagining. You will find yourself doing things that you may not have typically done. In time, you will bring into your life what you are looking for, and you will show yourself and the world what you are capable of.

Reflecting on my father's life, it is easy to recognize that his first big quantum leap was right after receiving *Think and Grow Rich* as a gift in 1961. It was that following year that his annual income became his monthly income. It was precisely that quantum leap that propelled him into this work. He became obsessed with discovering why he had changed so much – how he went from a self-described loser to what felt like overnight success in the 1960's. As he uncovered the answers, he then became obsessed with sharing that information with others.

Dad had many quantum leaps throughout his 60 years of teaching. But once he understood the principles of his success, he was no longer surprised by them. He had learned to operate from a place of expectation.

Here are the other 3 books at the top of my father's reading list. They are the ones stacked on his desk in his studio. They were sitting there, ready for the next trip he would take.

- *The Secret Of The Ages - by Robert Collier*
- *As A Man Thinketh - by James Allen*
- *The Power Of Awareness - by Neville Goddard*

Bob Proctor's library was extensive, and numerous other books could be on the list. However, these titles were the ones, in addition to *Think and Grow Rich* and *You²*, waiting on his desk.

CONSIDER...

What is it that you
most want to achieve?

Begin with a clear intention and see and feel yourself there, enjoying the life you desire. Basically, go there in your imagination and hold the image in your mind – your body and the Universe will catch up, matching that speed of vibration.

Decide you will consider other ways. You can do this by writing out the situation or circumstance and looking at it throughout the day. Then, add your thoughts each time you come back to it. Soon you will notice that you are expanding your thinking in new ways.

Don't skip this exercise, and definitely don't underestimate it. A sudden shift in consciousness can appear seemingly out of nowhere.

How can you bust free
from the limits you have been living with?

One step at a time. Keep your eye on your big picture and your big goal, and focus on the little things you can do each day that will add up to get you there.

Remember: Often, breakthroughs are made by violating logic. Bust free from limits by creating the habit of doing the illogical!

What do you need to change in your daily routine to put you on the path to your quantum leap?

Morning habits are an important part of your life to look at right now. If you want to change something about yourself and get different results, pay attention to what you focus on when you start your day; this sets the stage.

Take five minutes each morning and write out your goal. Include details. Write it in the present tense, and allow yourself to feel a strong sense of expectation. Though unseen to the naked eye, this sets up an attractive force.

Then, let this be the last thing you think of at night before falling asleep and the first thing you think of when you open your eyes in the morning. Take time to close your eyes and breathe into the feeling of having already achieved these things.

While you may or may not be aware of all the scientific and spiritual principles and universal laws being activated when you do this, please understand: This is how you create change in your life! Suspend your disbelief and trust the process.

In the morning, after you finish this exercise, write down two habits you want to make part of your new paradigm and work with them each day until they become your new routine. In the beginning, choose something that will quickly give you a taste of success. This could be as simple as making your bed right after you wake each day.

If your challenge is manageable at the start, you will likely stay committed, and you'll also get a taste of the discipline it will take. Then, as your belief grows stronger, so will your confidence in the idea that you are in the driver's seat and you can take on bigger changes.

Stay consistent. It might take a week, a month, or a year. That time will go by anyway, so use it to your benefit. It is repetition that will change your paradigms. Commit to that repetition. Remember: where attention goes, energy flows.

Get started right now. Your future self will thank you.

NOTES:

Dad loved being a father, grandfather,
and great grandfather

CHAPTER 12

SUPPORTING OTHERS

Be Present

"Let go of the past and enjoy the moment."
— Bob Proctor

In the early years of my life, while busy building a new business and trying to provide for our family, Dad still stopped and took the time to be present when we were together. We would spend time outdoors playing catch, and many weekends were spent together building a tree fort in the backyard of our home in Chicago. Whether night or day, I always felt valued and seen by Dad; even though I was young, I could feel his full attention.

In the *You Were Born Rich* recordings, Dad held up a sand timer and said, "You don't know how much time you've got left, and what's gone is gone; the only thing we have is right here and right now because the sand never stops running. This is all we've got, and to spend time now thinking about what happened in the past or worrying about the future is making certain we don't change anything. All you've got is now."

This was a lesson Dad shared with all of us as teenagers. Perhaps it was because a friend of his was killed in a car accident at the age of 16. If you'd have asked that young man on the morning he died how much time he thought he'd have left to live, he would have certainly said – a whole lot. That loss made an impression on my father that lasted his lifetime. He talked about it often and how it taught him to always appreciate the here and now.

During the summers, Dad would take me on the road with him when he worked. He would have me along to help in whatever way I could. He also wanted me immersed in the material and experience. I have fond memories of being on planes with him and long road trips in the car. He made sure I felt like I was contributing to the process, including me in conversations with influential people and making me feel valued – often asking my thoughts on something or asking me what I learned that day.

In those early years, I learned the value of relationships. I saw how Dad dealt with people while on the road and how he made sure that he left everyone he met feeling better because they met him.

When I started this chapter, it was during a visit to Toronto in 2019; I was staying at my Dad and Linda's home. As soon as my eyes opened each morning, I quickly got dressed and went to the sitting room, where I knew Dad would be waiting for me. We considered the mornings – "our time." We were the only ones awake, and it was still dark outside.

I'd pour myself a cup of coffee and top up his. He would greet me with a warm smile and a gentle touch. We'd sit quietly next to each other at the table. Dad would read *Think and Grow Rich*, just as he has done first thing every morning my entire life, and I was busy writing what you are holding in your hands.

We never needed to fill the space with words. I could feel his calm, loving energy as I sat beside him. And he could feel mine.

When we did begin to speak, Dad would ask me about this book. He'd ask questions that revealed his genuine interest; he'd listen intently, and offer me ideas. He was completely present and engaged in our conversation together.

As I write this now, I cannot help but think of the image of Dad holding that sand timer and saying we have no idea how much time we have. That lesson hits me differently now. And the truth is there are many lessons within that teaching.

We all knew my father was 87 years old and would not live forever, but it was impossible to imagine a world without him. Especially when you were with him. Even at the end, when he was not feeling well, he was fully present. Always giving and interested. Still curious and passionate.

It was easy to talk yourself out of the image that his health was deteriorating – and instead, focus on the idea that he would indeed continue to affect the world. That he would continue to be on the other end of the phone line each morning when I called.

But, of course, that is not the case. He is no longer physically here, but he is here. He is still affecting the world.

He is here in the man that I am. I see him in my children and grandchildren and hear him in the many clients who learned from him and the consultants he trained. Dad did change the world. And each of us is doing the same by sharing and living his message.

I have a chair in our master bedroom that looks out over Puget Sound. It is a leather recliner that Dad loved. It was 'his chair' whenever he visited our home in Florida. It is where I sit now to receive beyond my mind. I let my thinking mind fade into the background so I can receive from a greater source than myself. This is where I now sit and talk to my father.

CONSIDER...

How do you bring yourself to, and keep yourself in, the present moment?

The answer will be different for each of us, but there is a basic formula that peels away the noise.

1. *Consciously observe your thoughts and activities.*

2. *Stop and notice your surroundings.*

3. *Intentionally focus on just one thing.*

4. *Commit to setting aside distractions.*

5. *Be instead of Do.*

6. *Breathe.*

NOTES:

Speaking Good Behind People's Backs

" It doesn't matter where you are.
You are nowhere compared to
where you can go. "
— Bob Proctor

When Dad and I spoke each morning, we would intentionally talk good about the people in our lives. As the years rolled on, I came up with the phrase, 'Talking good behind their back.' I would bring up a name and say, "Let's talk good behind their back." Of course, he loved doing this.

He would frequently say to me, "You can always tell a person's character by what they say behind a person's back. Pay attention to what a person says and move away quickly if the conversation moves to negative energy about another person."

Too often, people get caught up in conversations that deal with trivial details or gossip and judgement. Getting dragged into that kind of energy is never a good thing. Instead, you can be the one talking good about someone when they are not in the room.

Pay attention to how it makes you feel. Watch how the person you are talking with comes to life. You will notice that you feel better about yourself and those around you. The positive energy you put out will return to you in ways that will surprise you.

Sometimes, you won't even make the connection. Until you do... that is when you know you are living in what is called *Praxis*, the alignment of belief with behavior. And that is a great way to live. You will be in a constant flow of good – both what you are putting out and what is flowing back to you.

Mike Dooley, an author, and speaker, said, "Thoughts become things, and your words are your wings." That caught my attention.

Be thoughtful with the words you speak. As Mike said, they are your wings. They can carry you to high places or take you to where you don't want to go.

Sometimes, after Dad and I would hang up, I would message the person we'd talked good about that day. I wouldn't give details; I would simply send a lovely little nugget of thought because that may be the one little thing to change the course of their day for the better.

Recently, I received a message out of the blue that did just that for me. The text said she and her husband were talking good about me behind my back. What a beautiful message. This means someone listened to my story and consciously chose to incorporate the practice into their life.

Sometimes I talk about those morning conversations with my father when I am speaking to a group. It brings me great satisfaction when I see eyes in the audience light up at the idea of making it a practice to speak behind someone's back in a positive and loving way.

Last week, I saw a fantastic post from the singer/songwriter Pink in the news. She said, "I'd like to propose a worldwide internet challenge to anyone reading this today. Go one day without criticizing someone online."

Pink has a large following, and that post may have made a positive difference for thousands of people in one day. But even if it only influenced one person – she made a difference. Because that one person will impact another. Imagine just for a moment how the world would be different if we all lived with that attitude.

The influence I strive to have in this world is by example. When we change ourselves first is when we will influence others through these teachings – one person at a time. The possibility of reach is infinite.

It is like that beautiful quote from Mahatma Gandhi:

> *"If we could change ourselves, the tendencies in the world would also change. As a man changes his own nature, so does the attitude of the world change towards him. We need not wait to see what others do. "*

CONSIDER...

How do you handle the 'rabbit hole' of negative or senseless chatter?

None of us are immune to getting caught up in this, but when you pay attention, you become aware of it much faster and can change the direction of the conversation – or change your direction and walk away. It is not always easy to walk the high road, but it is always better.

Give some thought to incorporating the practice of talking good about people. It is a Bob Proctor legacy that will continue to change the world.

Choose a friend and get them involved in this exercise with you. Have fun with it.

NOTES:

Impression Of Increase

"You should stand out like a beacon in a dark night! Think about what kind of positive influence you want to be in this world."
— Bob Proctor

When selling real estate in the late 1980's, I attended a large real estate conference in Palm Springs. During the event, the speaker asked me to come up to the stage. I had no idea what this was about, and it really surprised me. I was unprepared.

Once on stage, I was asked why I thought I was so successful in this business and quite successful right out of the gate. I thought for a moment, and then it hit me. I had formed the habit of doing something my father had taught me when I was young.

I was nine years old and about to start the fourth grade when we moved to Chicago. We had already moved several times in my young life – from Toronto to London and back to a different area in Toronto – and I was apprehensive about being the new kid once again. I was worried about how I would fit in.

I remember speaking with Dad about this in the den of our new home on Maplewood Lane in Glenview, Illinois. The advice he gave me all those years ago continues to affect how I treat and talk to people today.

The lesson I learned that day was what he referred to as 'The Impression of Increase.' It's about leaving everyone you interact with feeling better because they were in your presence.

Dad suggested that beginning on my first day at the new school, whenever I had the opportunity to speak to someone, I should use my imagination and see four letters across their forehead:

M.M.F.I. (Make Me Feel Important).

That acronym was to serve as a reminder to me to be present and interested. He would say, "It's a whole lot better to be interested than it is to be interesting."

He encouraged me to make eye contact and ask meaningful questions when I spoke with anyone. And he said that I needed to be genuine, and the only way to do that was to focus on the other person and not think about what I wanted to say next about myself. He explained what setting my ego aside meant and that my turn to be seen would come when I put the other person at ease.

He said, "Brian, there is good in everyone. Sometimes you must look a little harder with certain people, but it's always there, and if you look for it, you'll see it. And when you do see it, know that what you're seeing is a reflection of the good that's in you."

When I practiced this with intention, I noticed right away that I was making friends easily and people were comfortable in my presence.

So, when I was asked that day on stage what I thought had made me so successful, it was suddenly so obvious to me. It was that day in the den with Dad when I was nine years old. The tool he gave me really made sense to me, and since that day MMFI has shaped my way of being; it is how I automatically operate.

I realized that day on the stage that it was the reason for my instant and sustaining success in the real estate world and throughout my life. And with that realization, I decided to make it my mission to use 'The Impression of Increase' with intention.

Up to that point, I had been using it as an unconscious competent, and I knew I could harness its strength by consciously using MMFI.

To be successful at this, you must want the same for everybody that you want for yourself. And to do this authentically, you need to have respect and love for yourself.

The importance of self-love is weaved throughout this book. That is intentional.

I was taught that self-love is one of the most important things you'll ever do. By understanding, appreciating, and loving who you are, you will develop respect for yourself. You'll discover just how interesting, creative, and loveable you are, which will change your life. And when you change your life, you change the lives of those around you. The more we can love ourselves, the easier it is to love and accept others. It is easier to succeed at something if we have that base.

CONSIDER...

Self-love is your foundation
from which everything else is built.

The chatter in your mind will become more loving and patient as you practice being kind to yourself.

What do you commit to doing that will
make the people you encounter today feel better
because they were in your presence?

This does not need to be complicated, yet you may notice right away that despite the simplicity of these suggestions, they may still be challenging.

Take notice of that challenge. Don't judge yourself. Just notice where you have difficulties and know that this is an area in your life that needs more discipline and practice.

Everyone wants to feel 'seen.' And by using the MMFI exercise, you could make a difference in someone's life today.

1. *Make eye contact.*
2. *Smile.*
3. *Put your phone away.*
4. *Don't look around the room.*
5. *Listen.*
6. *Ask questions.*
7. *Sometimes, it can be as simple as giving a genuine compliment that shows you noticed.*
8. *Don't interrupt.*

When you practice MMFI, listen with genuine curiosity, speak honestly, and act with integrity.

NOTES:

Givers Gain

*"Willingly give and graciously receive.
What you do to and for another,
you do to and for yourself."*
— Bob Proctor

Are you a good giver? This is a question you would often hear Bob Proctor ask. When I would watch Dad willingly give to people, you could see them struggle to receive his generosity. And he would use that opportunity of awkwardness to point out that to be a good receiver, you must also be a good giver. They are two sides of the same thing.

This would often get me – and anyone else who was asked the question – thinking, "Am I a good giver? Do I willingly give my time, energy, resources, and attention?"

Giving was a way of life for my father, and he never expected anything from the people he gave to. He said that would be trading. So instead, he would say that good will return when you put good into the Universe. And you never know where that good will come from – but it will come. He had an unshakable understanding of this principle.

There was a book written by John David Mann & Bob Burg, *The Go-Giver*. Rumor was that the character Pindar in this book was based on my father. And when I read the book, I agreed Pindar could very well be Bob Proctor. Dad spent his life living the philosophy that *Givers Gain*. His example changed many lives.

One morning while talking with Dad, I asked him about the concept of giving. This is something that he was so incredibly good at. His response was simple and something that I had heard my entire life. Here is his answer word for word:

"Giving is one of the laws of the Universe. You've got to willingly give and graciously receive. If you have to think before you give, you are trading; you are not giving. When you give to someone else, you create an energy that will come back. You may not know where that good will come from, but it will come."

'Increase' is, without question, the natural urge of life seeking expression. So, when you are honestly attempting to leave everyone with more and better, people will quickly realize that by associating with you, they feel better. And what you are doing to and for others you are also doing to and for yourself.

Loving others is also loving yourself.

I have a good idea of why my father was such a good giver. He learned by example from his mother.

When he was a young boy during World War II, there were only a few men around as most were off fighting. My father, his sister, and his brother lived with their mother and grandmother in a neighborhood in Toronto where money was tight. Most people were just getting by.

Dad often shared a story about returning home from school one day and telling his mother about a family down the street that had run out of coal – they had no money to buy more. It was the dead of winter in Toronto, and most homes in the 1940's were heated with coal. Running out of coal would be dangerous in those winter temperatures.

My grandmother did not know who this family was, but the first thing she did was go to the can on top of the refrigerator, where she kept what little money she had. She gave a twenty-dollar bill to Dad and told him to go to the corner store and get it changed into two tens and to give the family ten dollars so they could buy a ton of coal to heat their home.

She did not have much money, and that ten dollars would have done a lot to help feed her own family. Yet, she was willing to help a family she didn't know.

Witnessing this selfless act as a young boy gave my father a glimpse of what it means to truly give. That ten dollars made a real difference for that family. His mother's act touched something inside of him that left an impression that lasted his entire life.

That loving generosity is something that came to define my Dad.

If you were to ask anyone close to Bob Proctor to describe him, the word 'generous' in one form or another would be used.

Dad taught me to live with a giving heart and treat others with kindness – not because they are kindhearted, but because I am. You can choose to live this way too.

As you think about giving and receiving, I would like to share with you a message that my father sent to my wife, Cory, in 2014. My father asked Cory to read this note every day when she woke. You may see yourself in his message; perhaps his words will help you too.

"Cory, I woke up thinking of you. I was thinking... you are a great mother, and then I thought... you approach everything the same way. You make certain all of your responsibilities are done exceptionally well. I also believe you do not permit the Universe to properly reward you. You are truly an exceptional woman, Cory, and I would like you to expect wonderful things to come into your life. Expect every aspect of your life to turn out as good as your children. You wanted them to turn out really well and you expected it to happen; I can tell that by the way you speak about Emma and Spencer. But on the occasions when I wanted to give you something, it was obvious that you found it difficult to accept it. I would love to see you become more aware of what a truly wonderful person you are and begin to expect the Universe to openly reward you. You do willingly give so much, but you do not graciously receive. It's almost as if your thoughts go to, 'oh no, I don't deserve all that.' You are a wonderful person – know that and expect greater good in your life.

These are my thoughts, Cory, and I wanted you to know. You are already aware that I am always right on these hidden matters. ;-)

I imagine you waking up, reading my message, and letting it sink in, causing you to become more aware of your tremendous inner good. Open up to all the good waiting for you. expect an abundance.

You must start to see what is so obvious to me. You must work at altering this paradigm. Take a few minutes each day before you get going. Sit quietly and do your Gratitude and at the top of the list, be grateful for the awareness of the sheer beauty that shines from you. Dwell on that and give thanks for it."

Bob Proctor

CONSIDER...

Are you a good giver?

When you give, you will gain by keeping it about your connection to people rather than from a desire to feel good about yourself.

As you give, you will see the flow return to you in unexpected ways, and your faith in this natural, lawful process will grow.

Are you a good receiver?

Giving and receiving are companion energies that take turns throughout our lives, and we all get a chance to be on both sides of that exchange. When you graciously receive, it is like a dance choreographed by universal laws. When you cannot graciously receive, you are robbing the giver of the opportunity of giving.

Notice how you feel when someone unexpectedly gives to you.

Think of a time you have offered support to someone.

How did it make you feel? Did you make an authentic heart-to-heart contact? When you feel this connection, you are connecting with the human experience. Imagine having more of that feeling.

There are many ways to give.

You can give in countless ways to add value to people's lives.

1. *Send thoughts of kindness, compassion, and goodwill to people who need it.*
2. *Make a phone call and check-in.*
3. *Smile at everyone you see.*
4. *Give away things you no longer need.*
5. *Offer a free service to provide for others.*
6. *Volunteer your time for those in need.*

You can undoubtedly think of many more ways to improve another person's day. Make your own list and pay attention to where you can add value.

What legacy do you want to leave?

Ultimately, you will be known for something. What do you want that to be? What would you like to do for others? Service towards something beyond ourselves gives our life meaning and brings it into balance.

To have true fulfillment, we must continue to grow and be willing to make life about more than just ourselves.

NOTES:

Gina

" Gina Hayden is the one that kept me in line.
I could not have done this without her."
— Bob Proctor

This book would not be complete without you hearing from this extraordinary woman. Gina Hayden worked side by side with my father for over 36 years. She is like a sister to me, and I am honored to call her a dear friend.

Why do I bring her up? For two reasons.

First and foremost, Gina, more than anyone, helped Bob Proctor craft his message for most of his career, and together, they developed many of Dad's programs that we all enjoy today.

Secondly, it is no mistake that she stood by Dad's side for such a long period of time.

You would often hear him say from the stage, "If you are in business and want to be more productive, and have success, then you need to get a Gina."

Over the years, I can think of many people who would come to us and say, "I found my Gina."

What does that mean? Dad believed that to be highly effective, you need to have someone by your side who can get things done. Gina was that person for Dad.

She is undoubtedly one of the most organized and effective individuals I have ever met. Gina and Dad became very close over those 36-plus years together. So close that when Gina got married, he walked her down the aisle and gave her away. That was a beautiful moment to witness.

As you can imagine, Gina could have moved on to do just about anything she wanted at any point during those 36 years. But instead, she chose to stay and work with Bob Proctor. That is a testament to the way he treated people and especially the way he treated her.

When I asked Gina if she would write a piece to include here, her eyes were welled with tears. You see, Gina is a part of our family, and like all of us, her life was profoundly shaped by having Bob Proctor in it and, more than anyone, by working so closely with him.

Gina's perspective is unique. She watched Bob Proctor's mind work and witnessed the process of how his creative genius unfolded.

My Bob

To have been asked to write this piece means more to me than I can express.

Bob Proctor earned an international reputation as one of the foremost thinkers of our time. He traveled the world, teaching people how to be more, do more, have more, and give more. But I think what he did better than anyone else: he taught people that abundance was their birthright and that life is to be enjoyed without guilt or judgement, and that it's to be lived in gratitude for everything we have.

By way of introduction, I met Bob Proctor in 1985 when I was working in Toronto. Our board of directors had asked Bob to help us fundraise for our gymnastics clubs. Bob's niece was a gymnast with one of our competitive clubs; Bob quickly agreed. I don't remember meeting him at the event, but he personally autographed a book for each of the staff. At that stage in my life, I didn't know any authors, and I surely didn't have any autographed books. We raised a lot of money because of the work Bob did for us, and later, I found out that he had donated all of his time for the three sessions of, "An Evening with Bob Proctor." Little did I know that this was the beginning of a beautiful relationship.

In July of 1986, I received an SOS from the gentleman who had helped bring Bob Proctor to our gymnastics community the year before and subsequently went to work with Bob. I was in between jobs, and he asked if I would come in to cover for someone. I suggested that I come in for a few weeks until they were able to hire someone for the position. Well, two weeks turned into 36 ½ years!

It's only in retrospect that I've realized how extraordinary Bob was. And, though I'd witnessed his humanity, kindness, and selflessness over the years, he was just, "My Bob!" He was everything and a bag of chips!

The next several paragraphs are a few of the lessons I took in along the way. Bob taught by example!

You can't give too much. *I don't know that I ever knew Bob to turn down an opportunity to help someone in need. I need to preface this because we, as staff in his company, had to turn down many requests on Bob's behalf over the years. But, if you happened to get through the gatekeepers and spoke to Bob directly, his natural response would have been YES!*

Make YOUR mark on the world. *Bob was a bit of a unicorn in that he spoke about a lot of things that were thought by many to be off-limits. He spoke openly about money and suggested it was a poor master but a great servant. He taught us that sex was a creative urge but that it could be quite destructive if you didn't harness that creative power. And God! He was speaking about God, Spirit, and Energy back in the early 70's when it was NOT a topic of discussion in companies. He paved the road for a lot of speakers, just as his mentor Earl Nightingale did for him. He was a trailblazer!*

Treat yourself well. *I learned quickly that it was best to sit in the front of the plane and back of the car and Bob afforded me the opportunity to do that, even in the early days when the company was struggling. I stayed where he stayed. I did not have a per diem. We ate together, and he always insisted I order whatever I wanted. That* *was foreign to me. I think sometimes he ordered something expensive, so my item seemed paltry even though it probably cost more than my whole family would have spent for a dinner out.*

Treat others as you wish to be treated. *We may look and act differently and have more or less money, but when it comes down to it, we're pretty much the same. It was an absolute joy to observe Bob; I learned so much. I watched how he was with people he knew and those he didn't. He always appeared interested, friendly and respectful. When we worked in hotels, he had the full cooperation and respect of all the hotel staff - the bellman, the kitchen staff, the servers, the banquet captains and whomever else we were dealing with. He always said please and thank you and made time for people. When we were working at a venue, anywhere in the world, the hotel staff went out of their way to get him anything he wanted which made my job a heck of a lot easier.*

A pro is at their best regardless. *This was Bob's credo. I remember an event in Los Angeles. It was a sold-out venue, and the room was packed. Bob was in his mid-eighties at the time. He was walking up the stairs to get back on the stage when he tripped and fell. It would have been easy for him to make a joke to lighten the mood, but he didn't. Instead, he got himself up, collected his thoughts and continued with his slides as if nothing had happened. I will never forget it. It was strength with style personified.*

What I want for myself, I want for others. *Bob enjoyed nice things. He wore tailored suits, custom-made shoes and shirts and always carried a good pen with him. He loved the way these things made him feel, but what he loved even more was gifting his staff and* *those close to him with the same things that made him happy. I think his tailor made more suits for our sales team than he made for Bob himself!*

In short, Bob was the man he showed to the world. *He wasn't perfect. But, he walked his talk. He expected an abundant life, and he received it graciously.*

To close, I want to share a story with you that I will never forget. We were in Los Angeles driving to the TV studio as Bob and other teachers from The Secret were going to be featured on Larry King Live. For me, this was a big deal. I looked at him and said, "Are you nervous?" He laughed and said, "Confidence is not something I lack." And then, in the next breath, he said, "I have been waiting for this my whole life." Bob always expected great things were going to happen to him. I still have the Larry King Live mug he received from the show that he gave to me. He was a rock star that night!

Bob Proctor, you led an extraordinary life and I learned from you every single day. I miss you, my friend.

Gina Hayden

Larry King with Dad

Nan, Dad and Linda

NOTES:

CHAPTER 13

THE END

It's Time To Take Action

*"Discipline is the ability to give yourself
a command and follow it."*
— Bob Proctor

At the book's beginning, I asked, "What will happen in your life if you show up as the best version of yourself?"

It is time to reflect on that question again. I have had great successes in my life and my fair share of failures as well. And for as long as I can remember, it was my father who kept me on track. He would say to me, "Do what you can today. You can't change what happened yesterday. Yesterday was decided based on the information you had at that moment. Tomorrow is the future. What you have is right now."

So, it doesn't matter whether your past is a story of success or failure. What matters is how you show up in the moments in front of you. Know your strengths, love yourself, and have an image of where you want to go as a person and contributor in this world. When I was young and would achieve great success, it would bother me that after saying congratulations, the first thing Dad would ask me was, "What's next?" He never made a big deal of success. Instead, he kept me focused on the moment and reaching forward.

As an adult, when he asked me that question, I realized it was my ego that wanted recognition. He was right. Keep looking and moving forward because living this way will get you through times of great difficulty. Don't risk getting stuck in a single moment of glory. Instead, choose growth. Enjoy your moment, set a new goal, and look for where you can provide service and value – focus outward. Make that who you are. You continue growing by committing to a life of study and taking action with the knowledge you are gaining. Stay curious!

Dad would often quote Billy Graham:

> *"The smallest package in the world is the person that's all wrapped up in themselves. People who are most successful are the ones who really care about other people".*

He would remind me of this to ensure I always kept the main thing, the main thing. Helping others.

It is also essential to look at the good around you, thank yourself for how far you have come, be grateful for yourself, and harness the belief that you can go as far as you desire.

Personal growth has no finish line. Stretching for improvement keeps us energetic. It keeps us alive and relevant. Each day holds an unlimited number of possibilities, and small steps add up to significant accomplishments.

The book you are reading is an excellent example of that. I did not sit down and write it all at once. I simply did a little each day, and those days added up until I felt that I had something worth sharing.

When my father wrote *You Were Born Rich*, he did so by getting up an hour earlier each day and writing for one hour. Those single-hour segments added up to over nine 40-hour workweeks of focused attention in just one year.

Not long ago, Peggy McColl was holding an event in Sarasota, Florida. She asked me to come and share some stories from the stage. She specifically wanted me to share lessons I learned growing up with Bob Proctor.

I mention this now because we are talking about taking action. As I was on the stage, something I had never shared before came out of me. "Sometimes it is more important to take imperfect action than to plan for perfection."

I have seen so many people plan and plan and plan but never step out and do. Yet, I have seen others willing to step out, and take 'imperfect action,' and accomplish greatness. Risking failure with imperfect action can be a beautiful part of the process.

Rewards in life are usually closer than you think. You will instinctively know when you are on the right track with an idea; you will feel it. Feeling is the language of the subconscious mind. And when you reach that point, you will know you have planted the idea into your subconscious mind.

Bob Proctor was known for making decisions quickly; he would promptly take the first step and plan the rest as it unfolded. Of course, it didn't always work out for him. But many times, it did, and it worked out well. He would have been the first to tell you that his failure stories were as important as his success stories.

Dale Carnegie summed it up nicely when he said, "Inaction breeds doubt and fear. Action breeds confidence and courage. If you want to conquer fear, do not sit at home and think about it. Go out and get busy."

I hope you have found something in this book that has resonated with you or sparked a desire that encourages you to stretch for new heights.

My goal with this book has been to help you in any small or significant way to live a better life, but also, it is a way for me to honor the incredible man that was my father.

The spirit never dies. Tap into the wisdom of Bob Proctor. Do like I do: sit in a quiet space, and ask him questions.

Before I say goodbye for now, I want to share one last thing with you. In the chapter 'Father's Day,' I wrote about the day we placed Dad's urn into its final resting place. As you can imagine, choosing a quote to forever live on the stone marking his resting place was no simple task. Dad loved quotes and believed they carried tremendous meaning and power.

However, we landed on one that is perfect.

PROCTOR

Robert "Bob" Corlett

July 5, 1934 - February 3, 2022

"The great use of life is to spend it for something that will outlast it."

- William James

CONSIDER...

What can you do today
to bring you closer to your goal?

If you're serious about wanting significant changes in your life, you need to take action. Even if it is for only 10 minutes, it all adds up. And when you feel good about yourself, you end up being more, doing more, and having more. The universe is willing to give you whatever you want. So, stay in harmony with it by staying focused and taking small steps each day.

The following question was asked at the beginning of this book. I hope that by reading these pages, it is a question that you have now given some serious thought to. Life is too short to show up as anything other than our best. I also hope that by reading these pages, you understand that you are capable of so much more than you have allowed yourself to imagine. Change comes from within, and that is the same for all of us. We are all works in progress.

WHAT WILL HAPPEN IN YOUR LIFE
IF YOU SHOW UP AS THE
BEST VERSION OF YOURSELF?

NOTES:

ACKNOWLEDGEMENTS

First and foremost, I want to thank my wife, Cory Kelly Proctor. You have been my rock! Your encouragement to keep going and finding ways to support me in getting this book written is appreciated more than words could ever describe.

You were able to take my words and add color and texture to my message. The best way I can describe it is that I built the house, and you decorated it. The time you took on this and how you brought the best out of me has given us both something to be proud of. This book would not be what it is without you.

I know how happy Dad was that we found each other. You have enhanced my life and knowing that I get to spend each day with you brings me immense joy.

My two children, Danny and Leanne: You show me every day in the way you treat those around you what it is like to leave everyone with the impression of increase. I am so proud of you both.

My two step-children, Spencer and Emma: You both have welcomed me into your life with such warmth and love. You have taught me unconditional acceptance. I am so grateful to have become a part of your family.

My friend Peggy McColl: I appreciate your guidance and help in making this book possible. You are every author's friend.

My friend Trace Haskins: You have helped me navigate the technical side of all of this by bringing my book and website to the world in a clear and comfortable way. You have made all of this easy.

My family: There are too many of you to mention by name, but each one of you has inspired different parts of what is written here. I wouldn't be who I've become without you, nor would this book have taken the form it has taken.

Last but definitely not least, you – the reader. I thank you for reading this book and dedicating a portion of your life to personal growth. Thanks to you, these lessons have a chance to live on and expand forever – and you add your own unique magic touch to each of them. Thank you, and enjoy the rest of this beautiful life.

ABOUT THE AUTHOR

Brian Proctor

Brian was born in 1961, the same year that his legendary father, Bob Proctor, was given the book *Think and Grow Rich by Napoleon Hill*, which began his father's 60-year journey into personal development.

For close to 30 years, Brian had the privilege of working alongside his father as he taught from some of the world's largest stages, and for 60 years they were best friends.

While working with his Dad, Brian found his niche in marketing and business development. In the very early years of the Internet, Brian originated a powerful idea to build an email list by creating value which morphed into a massive worldwide platform for his father to share his teachings. This idea set Bob Proctor's company up for success by opening the door early to email list building long before that became the industry standard.

As an online marketer, Brian was consistently the top affiliate in many large product launches with joint ventures, bringing in millions of dollars in commissions for himself and his father's organization as well as giving many entrepreneurs their first opportunities to share their products and services with a large audience.

Brian attributes his success to all the lessons he has learned over the years from his father.

Today, Brian enjoys his role as co-founder of KellyProctorCo LLC, an organization created with his wife, Cory Kelly Proctor, whose mission is to empower people to live their best life by leaning into simple yet profound strategies.

They live at the south end of Puget Sound in Washington state and are enjoying their dream of a life spent living near the water and enjoying nature at its finest.

Brian is honored to continue helping people just like you create lives, careers and businesses you love, living the good life on your own terms, and showing you how building relationships, making a difference and creating wealth fit together.

To learn more from Brian and/or his programs, visit:

www.brianproctor.com

Printed in Great Britain
by Amazon

25122445R00203